IMAGES OF ENGLAND

BURTON UPON TRENT PUBS

IMAGES OF ENGLAND

BURTON UPON TRENT PUBS

DAVID MOORE AND GRAHAM COXON

TEMPUS

Frontispiece: Ariel view of Burton town centre in the 1960s, with New Street in the foreground. There have been over seventy pubs in the town centre. Today there are just twelve, plus two hotels and a few bar restaurants.

First published 2004

Tempus Publishing Limited
The Mill, Brimscombe Port,
Stroud, Gloucestershire, GL5 2QG
www.tempus-publishing.com

© David Moore and Graham Coxon, 2004

The right of David Moore and Graham Coxon to be identified
as the Author of this work has been asserted in accordance
with the Copyrights, Designs and Patents Act 1988.

British Library Cataloguing in Publication Data.
A catalogue record for this book is available from the British Library.

ISBN 0 7524 3255 9

Typesetting and origination by Tempus Publishing Limited.
Printed in Great Britain.

Contents

Acknowledgements

We would like to thank everyone who has provided the information and photographs that have made the compilation of this book so interesting and enjoyable. Particular thanks go to Glenys Cooper and Ottakars, *Staffordshire Newspapers Ltd.*, Graham Nutt and David Feltham of the Magic Attic (*Burton Mail* archives), David and Keith Gilliver, Valerie Burton and the Burton Civic Society, Burton Library, Eric Fower and Bruce Woodford, Thelma Barrell and Coors Visitor Centre (formerly Bass Museum), and Tutbury Chapel Antiques. Also Roy Agar, Dave Bodell, Brearleys Antiques, Walter Cooper, Roy Edwards, Arthur Emmerson, Richard Farman, Terry Garner, Simon Gaskin, Stuart Haywood, Faith Hudson, Mick Lewis, Kevin McDonald, 'Spadge' Mayger, Andrew Myrtle, Kevin Neale, the Newey grandchildren, Wendy Ogden, David Pantry, Mrs B.A. Phillips, Arthur Roe History 2000.co.uk, David Stacey, Nikky and Carl Stout, Tony Tomlinson, Margaret Dawson, Peter Turner, Barry Weaver, David Wright and Michael Wright, not forgetting the people who took the photographs in the first place, even those whose memories may have been playing tricks! Mostly, thanks must go to the landlords and landladies of Burton, past and present.

Bibliography

Molyneux W, *Burton-on-Trent; its History, its Waters and its Breweries*. Trubnor & Co. 1869
Owen C.C, *The Greatest Brewery in the World* Derbyshire Record Society Vol.1. 1992
Owen C.C, *The Development of Industry in Burton-on-Trent*. Phillimore & Co. Ltd. 1978
Stuart D, *History of Burton upon Trent*. Chartered Trustees of Burton upon Trent. 1975.
Underhill C.H, *The History of Burton upon Trent*. Tresises. 1976.
Underhill C.H, *Here and There*. Tresises. 1980.

Introduction

The Abbot of Burton brewed good ale
On Fridays when he fasted
But the Abbot of Burton ne'er tasted his own
So long as his neighbour's lasted

Burton upon Trent has often been described as the brewing capital of England. This is not altogether surprising, with so many breweries in the town at one time or another producing outstanding products and assisted, as all Burtonians know, by that bit of luck which resulted in something special finding its way into the water! With such a brewing heritage, perhaps it should come as no surprise to find that there has never been a shortage of public houses in the town. It would be a brave person who would say with certainty exactly how many there have been, but claims of one for every day of the year appear to be optimistic. Nevertheless, it is possible to identify around 270 pubs, inns, taverns and traditional hotels altogether, although it seems that at no time have there been more than 200.

The purpose of this book is not to merely trace and record as many as possible, but also to celebrate the public houses of the town, past and present. In short, it is to appreciate the pleasure they have given. Attractive as the idea was, we have resisted the temptation to include hostelries in the nearby villages. Instead we have confined ourselves to those lying roughly within an area bounded by the old corporation bus routes: the town centre pubs as well as the so-called back-street boozers; up to the Acorn at Rough Hayes and as far as the Beacon Hotel along Tutbury Road, including the whole of Winshill and Stapenhill and along Branston Road, as far as the Branston Arms and up to the Derby Inn on Derby Road. We have looked at traditional hotels too, particularly those dating back to the days of the coaching inns, but we have not included what were sometimes referred to as beer sellers or beer retailers, many of which were similar to what later became known as off-licences. Most of those didn't have a pub name; records normally indicated only who the licence holder was and the address, often a private house. Nor have we concerned ourselves with social clubs or licensed bars not open to the general public.

Although the Three Queens Hotel, which dates back to 1531, is often regarded as being the oldest hostelry in Burton, probably followed by High Street's Old Crown Inn and the Bulls Head near the corner of High Street and New Street near to what was known as the Abbey gateway, there is some evidence that the most ancient could well be a licensed premises called the Swan-on-the-Hoop, described as being situated 'between the tenements of William de Peek and Dom. Thomas de Gresley, Knt. and abutting on the King's Way'. In other words its exact location is something of a mystery. Nevertheless, the hostelry, ruled by the Burton Abbey, is thought to have dated back to 1397 and was last mentioned in 1454.

According to Charles Underhill in his *History of Burton upon Trent*, there were forty-six licensed victuallers in Burton in the year 1604 when the population of the town was around 1,500. Then, even more than now, they were often the centre of social life. Records from 1818 indicate that there were thirty-four inns and taverns in Burton town centre as well as three coaching inns, the Three Queens, the Old Crown and the George. There were a handful of pubs on the outskirts of town too, in Stapenhill and Winshill for instance, two villages which in those days were not regarded as being in Burton itself, but were in fact part of Derbyshire. Of those thirty-seven hostelries in the town centre, just six remain today. These are the Three Queens Hotel, Blue Posts, Anchor Inn, Dog Inn, and the Royal Oak in the Market Place, plus the Fox and Goose in Bridge Street, now known as the Bridge Inn. On the site of one of the town's oldest pubs, the Star Inn in High Street, stands a bar restaurant called The Lounge, the sixth licensed premises on that site.

By 1880 there were approximately 160 public houses and hotels in the town, and this was increasing. There were so many pubs around at that time that some landlords had other jobs to ensure their families had a decent standard of living and often the licence was in the wife's name. With a population of just under 40,000, there was, on average, one licensed premises for every 250 or so inhabitants. As it was unusual to see women in public houses, and there was a substantial number of people under drinking age, the ratio was probably more like one for every hundred potential imbibers.

By 1911 the number of pubs was beginning to reduce; records indicate there were 145. Eighty-eight pubs had full licences, and fifty-seven were beer houses. There were six hotels too. Inevitably, since then, many Burton pubs have been demolished. Others have been turned into shops or private houses. Some have had their names changed, some recently with the advent of theme pubs, and others much earlier. A few have reverted to their original name or something similar.

Nevertheless, even as recently as 1960, there were around 130 pubs trading. Sadly, since then, another fifty have disappeared although the rate of decline has slowed with just seven closing since 1987. Three of them were Marstons' houses: the Freehold Tavern in Stapenhill, the Waggoners Inn, the last public house in Horninglow Street to survive, and the Forest Gate in Moor Street. Three Bass houses have been lost too: the Avenue, a prefabricated pub in Horninglow, the Gate Inn on Tutbury Road and the Napier Arms. There was also one Ind Coope pub, the Queens Arms on West Street in Winshill. Today there are just over eighty public houses in Burton plus a few traditional hotels and a sprinkling of bar restaurants.

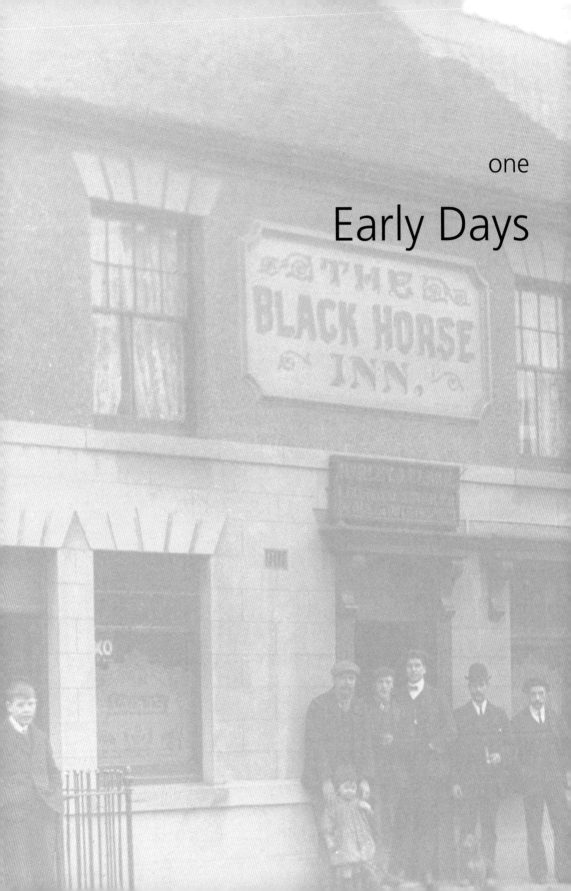

one

Early Days

The monks knew all about beer and justified brewing and drinking it on the grounds that it was a valuable source of nutrients. It was safe to drink as well, as beer is incapable of sustaining organisms that cause disease. Of course, it probably made their existence a little more enjoyable too! Unfortunately for them, it wouldn't have been consumed in a warm and cosy public house as it was almost 400 years before the first pub-like venues came into existence.

The excellence of Burton beer is often attributed to the special qualities of the water drawn from wells, notably its hardness due to the underground gypsum deposits. Early on, with transportation difficulties, most of it was drunk locally. In Burton, as in other towns, the vast majority of pubs brewed their own beer and sold it on the premises. Only later did they start to supply their products to other houses and, when the Trent Navigation opened, it was possible for the brewers of the town to trade further afield. As well as the 'brew pubs', there were other groups of people involved in ensuring that the working man was able to get his pint when he needed to. Some were described as beer sellers or beer retailers, often purchasing beer from the small breweries and then selling it from their own house.

Left: An arrangement of bygone pub items.

Opposite: The Abbey Inn on Manor Drive. Set in picturesque surroundings overlooking the River Trent. It was in this location that the monks began brewing beer in Burton. Home to the Burton Club, for many years it was a Bass house.

Left: A variety of architectural styles of Burton pubs from a series of beer mats produced by Ind Coope.

Opposite: A group of beer mats advertising beers from Burton breweries.

By 1851, there were twenty-five commercial brewers in Burton. Due to the excellent reputation of Burton-brewed ales, brewing companies from other towns and cities also built breweries in the town. Truman's, the London brewer, bought Phillips Brewery in Derby Street and Charrington moved in too; their Abbey Brewery was next to what is now the Leopard Inn in Lichfield Street. The Charrington name returned decades later when the company merged with Bass, and a few regional breweries like Walkers of Warrington decided to brew some of their products in Burton. Henry Boddington of Manchester opened their brewery near the Cricketers Arms in Meadow Road off the Burton Bridge. Everard's of Leicester came to the area as well, initially in Meadow Lane and later at their Anglesey Road brewery.

Today there are five breweries in the town. The biggest is the massive Coors operation on site of the old Bass and Carlsberg-Tetley breweries. For over 200 years, Bass and Burton

EVERARDS
Tiger Bitter

Revives a great
British taste
1666
BEN
TRUMAN
EXPORT PALE ALE
SIR BENJAMIN TRUMAN

Worthington
Bitter

INDCOOPE'S
BURTON
ALE
BREWED AT BURTON

Marston's
Traditional Draught Beers

BREWED IN BURTON

were synonymous. To the thousands who worked for the famous brewing company, it was a way of life, whilst today Bass is just a brand owned by the Belgian brewer Interbrew. Marstons, an important part of Wolverhampton and Dudley Breweries, still prospers and there are three micro breweries in the town too. Two of them, the Burton Bridge and the Old Cottage, have their own outlets, the third, the Tower Brewery in Wharf Lane, hasn't. Coors can brew more beer in half a day than the other three combined produce in a year.

It was around the beginning of the twentieth century that breweries began to build or acquire their own public housing estates. Until then, most pubs were not salubrious, and drunkenness was widespread. Not surprisingly, Burton's breweries were in the forefront of these fundamental changes.

By far the largest number of pubs in Burton have been owned by Bass, including many Worthington pubs as well as those of Marstons and Ind Coope. Bass, who started brewing in Burton in 1777, increased the size of their pub estate in the town in early 1927 by merging with Worthington & Co. who themselves had a substantial number of houses. A few months later they purchased the business of T.F. Salt & Co. whose brewery in High Street closed soon afterwards and, six years later, bought James Eadie & Co., their brewery in Cross Street soon becoming surplus to requirements.

Ind Coope began brewing in Burton in 1858 and for many years their brewery stood next to that of Allsopp's in Station Street. In 1934, the two amalgamated. Earlier, Ind Coope was associated with three other Burton brewers, Bindley's, Robinson's and the Burton Brewery Co. Despite that, and surprising considering the size of its brewing operation, Ind Coope, later Allied Breweries, always had a relatively small number of pubs in the town although their estate did increase as a result of the 1978 pub swaps.

Back in the late nineteenth century, Marstons decided to increase the number of their public houses in the town and a merger with Nunneleys of Bridge Street in 1888 and A.H. Yeomans in 1890 went some way to achieving this. Eight years later they amalgamated with John Thompson & Co. and in 1900 bought Burton brewers Beard Hill & Co.

One of the Bass bottle cars.

Above and overleaf: A selection of beer mats which advertise the Burton Breweries.

White Shield—the original pale ale that matures in the bottle.

White Shield is one of the very last beers brewed in this traditional manner—certainly no other ale has its distinctive, slightly dry and nutty flavour.

The natural fermentation produces a little natural sediment. For this reason the bottle should not be shaken before opening. Pour with bottle and glass at eye level and leave the last tablespoonful of beer with the sediment behind. Encourage head to form as you pour.

TO THE TRADE ONLY.

IND COOPE & ALLSOPP LIMITED
BURTON BULK ALES

As and from 19th April, 1943, until further notice.

		Price per Hhd.	Price per Brl.	Price per Kil.	Price per Fir.	Public Bar Retail Price per Pint
D	—Pale Ale ...	... 231/-	154/-	77/-	38/6	1/4
BB	—Bitter Ale ...	... 195/-	130/-	65/-	32/6	1/2
B	—Bitter A...	... 168/-	112/-	56/-	28/-	1/-
No. 3	—Strong Ale ...	... 231/-	154/-	77/-	38/6	1/4
XXX	—Mild Ale ...	... 168/-	112/-	56/-	28/-	1/-
XX	—Mild Ale ...	... 138/-	92/-	46/-	23/-	11d.
X	—Light Mild Ale	... 117/-	78/-	39/-	19/6	10d.

Burton-on-Trent.   *19th April, 1943.*

THE ABOVE PRICES ARE SUBJECT TO A SURCHARGE OF:—

    130/- PER BARREL NET FOR X and XX.
    134/- PER BARREL NET FOR B.
    136/- PER BARREL NET FOR XXX.
    158/- PER BARREL NET FOR BB.
    178/- PER BARREL NET FOR D and No. 3.

ALL PREVIOUS LISTS ARE CANCELLED.

Right: An Ind Coope & Allsopp price list from 1943. Prices are shown for hogsheads (54 gallons), barrel (36 gallons), kilderkin (18 gallons) and firkins (9 gallons) as well as public bar prices for a pint, ranging from 10d (around 4p) to 1s 4d (around 7p).

mainly to acquire their pubs. Five years after that they amalgamated with Sydney Evershed Ltd, who had a brewery in Bank Square to form Marston Thompson & Evershed Ltd. In 1926, when Charrington & Co. decided to cease their operations in Burton and concentrate on their business back in London, Marstons purchased all of their pubs in Burton.

London brewers Truman came to town in 1873 and, although they continued to brew in Burton until 1970, during that time they acquired just five pubs, all of them relatively close to their Derby Street brewery. They acquired Everard's of Leicester, but never had more than one town pub, the Albion Vaults in High Street purchased in 1936 and sold in 1962.

By the 1920s, brewers had begun investing large sums of money in their public houses. Some new pubs were built too, usually bigger and better than the ones they were replacing, which were often sold to help fund the new ones. Most were tenanted but some were managed houses. It wasn't until the early 1960s that customers began to expect better facilities. The availability of food suddenly became an issue and some pubs began to offer entertainment and music. With the introduction of keg beers and lagers there had to be improvements in cellars and beer-dispense equipment. In some houses, but by no means all, the decor and furnishings needed to reflect the changing times. Over the next two decades, there was a move back towards the more traditional pub, although the 'wooden' beams were likely to have been made of something rather different. Then came the relatively brief period when theme pubs became fashionable, and now, of course, we have the town centre wine and café bars.

Advertisements for two of the town's latest micro breweries.

Pubs were different fifty years ago – they were a man's world – a place where you could go to get away from the women and talk about football. I didn't go to a pub to sup pints all night. Popping into my local gave me a chance to see my friends, hear the news and talk about things only men would find interesting.

This unknown patron paints a vivid picture of a typical pub at the time and, of course, there are pubs like that today. At one time, the idea of having a meal in a public house was totally alien. Instead, the staple was a bag of crisps and later a cob from under a glass dome at the end of the bar. Pubs were places to chat with your friends. They were somewhere to celebrate a win or drown your sorrows after your team had lost again.

The pub needed a good landlady or landlord to look after regulars and beer with equal care and attention, and was as likely to be found in the cellar as the bar. The cellar was rarely seen by customers but was assumed to be clean with the beer being properly looked after – not too fresh, not too old. Traditional cask-conditioned draught beer was properly pegged and kept at the correct temperature. Often only the landlord knew exactly what went on in the cellar.

Over the years, it's unlikely that many Burtonians would have described themselves as connoisseurs, but most knew their beer and still do. Despite the best efforts of the

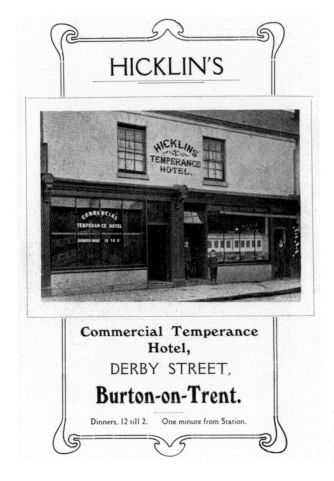

HICKLIN'S

Commercial Temperance Hotel,
DERBY STREET,
Burton-on-Trent.

Dinners, 12 till 2.   One minute from Station.

Temperance hotels in the brewing capital of England? This one was situated in Derby Street. It didn't last too long!

marketing men, beers with thick, creamy heads weren't particularly popular with the Burton beer drinker; it wasn't unusual for a miffed customer to return his pint if it had a few bubbles on the top.

As far as the perfect beer was concerned, a full pint of clear amber nectar with a distinct taste and aroma of hops was the most important thing. It was, of course, to be served at the right temperature, usually through a hand-pump, although it sometimes came straight from the cask. The chances were a customer's first beer in the pub wouldn't have been their first of the day. Most of the many people who worked for one of the town's breweries could also well have sunk a few pints of allowance to replace the sweat during a hard day's work.

Years ago, choosing a local pub probably depended on three things. Of initial importance was the convenience of location. Normally, it would have to be within easy walking distance, although this was unlikely to be a problem with so many to choose from spread evenly through the town. Secondly, the pub should offer good, convivial company, perhaps accompanied by a game of dominoes or darts and, thirdly, a good glass of ale. One thing was certain, a landlord who didn't serve a decent pint wouldn't last long. Whereas a landlord might not be able to improve the product, he could quite easily ruin it.

A small crowd has gathered outside the Black Horse in Moor Street to have their photograph taken.

Pubs and the Law

Pubs and beer have always attracted a great deal of legislation. Much of it is concerned with raising revenue, some of it aiming to control excessive consumption, others to regulate the brewing industry and the way its products are sold to the public. In fact there have been laws governing the production, sale and consumption of beer since the early thirteenth century. Almost 500 years later in 1786, when drunkenness was perceived as a serious problem, there was a Royal Proclamation which had the effect of reducing the number of licensed premises and may have encouraged the drinking of beer rather than stronger products. Forty-four years later in 1830, the Beerhouse Act came into force, its main purpose being 'the better supplying of the public in England with beer'.

The 1830 Act was not particularly successful. Large numbers of beerhouses opened as the justice system had little or no powers to control them. They could sell beer for an annual fee of two guineas and there was no excise duty. This encouraged the growth of what became known as beer sellers and retailers who often bought beer from small local brewers and sold it from their homes. In 1869 the Licensing Act resulted in better control of new excise licenses and the rapid rise in the number of beerhouses stopped. Then, in 1904, another piece of legislation, the Compensation Act, allowed magistrates to close pubs for reasons other than that of a landlord considered unfit to run the establishment. Compensation, funded mainly by brewing companies, was paid to the tenant and the owner.

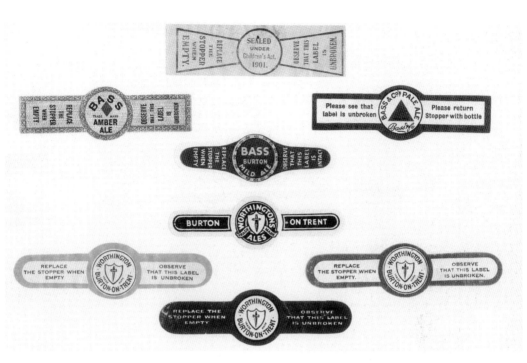

A selection of beer bottle top seals required by law for children carrying alcoholic beverages.

A selection of brewery memorabilia to remind us of days gone by.

David Lloyd George, Minister of Munitions, told parliament during the First World War that 'drinking is doing more damage than all the German submarines put together'. What followed was the Defence of the Realm Act (DORA) which gave the government more control over licensing hours, advertising, and strength of beer (which was reduced). The excise duty was also increased. A total ban was considered but rejected on the grounds that it would be bad for morale. It would have been pretty bad for the Chancellor of the Exchequer too! The DORA restrictions lingered on for many years after the war had ended. Around that time, prohibition and temperance groups had been doing their best to exert influence across the country but, not surprisingly, they found little support in Burton, neither from the brewery owners nor the working man – full employment in the town relied to a large extent on a successful brewing industry. An interesting find by a noted scientist around that time discovered that a bushel of barley processed through a brewery into beer produces more nutrition than the same amount of barley processed through a pig and eaten as pork. This helped put a stop to the beer rationing which had been encouraged by the Temperance movement.

Between 1969 and 1989, there were fifteen official reports into the brewing industry. In 1969, the Monopolies Commission concluded that the tied house system was a bad thing and nine years later there were a series of pub swaps across the country. In Burton, old-established Bass houses suddenly began to offer Allied Brewery products to its rather bemused customers. A regular at the Station Hotel used to his pint of draught Bass would suddenly be offered a glass of Ind Coope bitter instead. In fact, half a dozen Bass houses, including the Royal Oak in the Market Place, the Devonshire and the Gladstone, transferred across to Ind Coope. This resulted in Bass owning thirty-six houses in Burton, all but six of them tenancies. Their managed houses were the Blue Posts, the Derby Turn Inn, the Jubilee in Hawfield Lane, the popular Locomotive in Station Street as well as the Abbey Inn and Midland Hotel. Ind Coope's estate suddenly increased to sixteen including four managed houses: the Crown in Rosliston Road, the Roebuck opposite the brewery in Station Street, the Royal Oak in the Market Place, and the Station Hotel. Marstons had twenty-six pubs then, three of which were managed: the Albion Hotel, New Talbot Hotel and the Star and Garter. Around that time, the regulars at the five Truman's pubs in Burton, the Prince Alfred, Hanbury Arms, Rose and Crown, Black Eagle and the British Oak, found themselves sampling the products of John Smith's Tadcaster brewery after the London brewer dispensed with its pub estate in the town.

The Beer Orders, which followed an investigation into the brewing industry in the United Kingdom by the Monopolies and Mergers Commission in 1989, fundamentally changed the whole brewing industry after Lord Young at the Department of Trade and Industry said he 'was minded to accept their recommendations'. The result turned out to be something of a compromise and Lord Young finished up upsetting nearly everybody when he announced that each of the six big national brewers had to remove the tie from 50 per cent of their pubs over the first 2,000 they owned, and had to sell at least one guest beer which had to be cask conditioned. This prompted monumental changes in the brewing industry, which changed the relationship between brewing companies and their retail outlets. Some brewers were compelled to sell thousands of their outlets, usually to pub companies which suddenly sprung up. Whether it has improved the choice of products for the consumer is debatable. It has certainly done little to reduce the price of a pint across the country. Fifteen years later, instead of six UK brewers owning 77 per cent of the market, four brewers own almost exactly the same proportion, much of it in foreign hands.

MIDLAND HOTEL

STATION STREET

AND

GUILD STREET

TELEPHONE No. 2723

FUNCTIONS AND PARTIES OF ALL DESCRIPTIONS
IN THE NEW ASSEMBLY ROOM

Bass **Worthington**

ON DRAUGHT AND IN BOTTLE

38

An advertisement for
the Midland Hotel.

Today many traditional pubs struggle to survive. Landlords find it difficult to attract young customers. Those specialising in catering are doing better, whilst many of the trendier bars targeting the affluent younger drinker are thriving – good luck to them. Pubs can't compete with the supermarket prices and so many people are drinking at home. You'll certainly save a lot of money if you do but it's not quite the same as popping down for a couple of pints at your local. Ask any English men or women living abroad what they miss the most and there's a fair chance their answer will be 'a visit to the pub', even more than a jar of Marmite! The old adage seems to be true of pubs as well, 'use them or lose them'.

Liz Stone and Dave Hinchcliffe outside The Tavern, Borough Road. Opened in February 1993, and lasting for only two to three years, was this Burton's most short-lived pub?

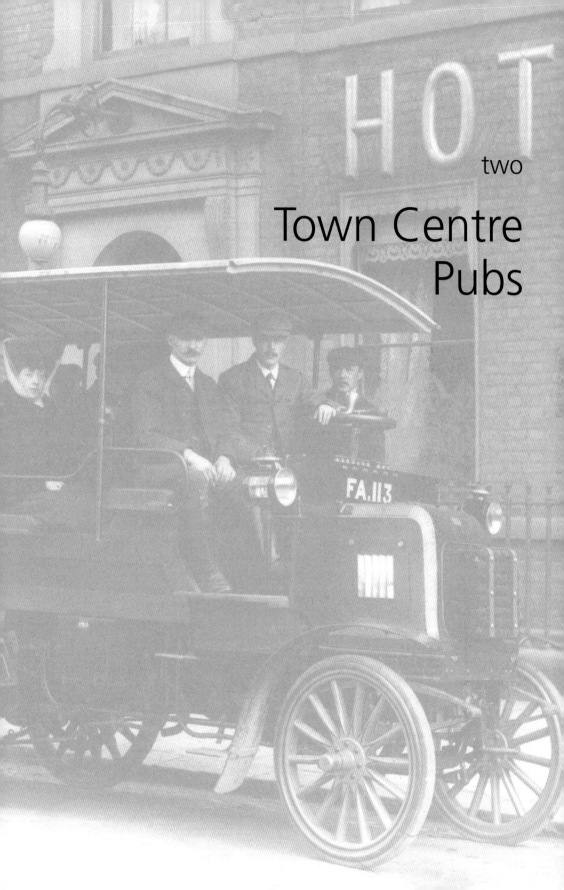

two

Town Centre
Pubs

Not surprisingly, most of the old pubs of Burton have been situated in the town centre, along High Street into the Market Place and across the road into Bank Square. Moving on to what was known as Bond End, including Green Street, Abbey Street, Fleet Street and Lichfield Street. From here, along Station Street as far as the railway station, are Guild Street, Union Street, New Street, Horninglow Street and Bridge Street.

One of the best indications that there were a substantial number of pubs in Burton in the late eighteenth century is a 1789 list of locals in the town centre. According to Charles Underhill's *Here and There*, there were seventeen altogether. Eight of those were in High Street, Ye Star, run by a Wm. Stanley, White Horse (W. Dimilow), Nag's Head (Richard Wilson), the strangely spelt White Lyon (Ant. Burton), White Hart (Thos. Wilson), Wheat Sheaf (Ricd. Warren), Blue Posts (Geo. Yeomans) and Ye Boot.

There were five in New Street, Ye Anchor (Jno. Sanders), King of Prussia (Hen. Shorthose), Carpenter's Arms (Wm. Waite), Queen's Head (W. Dyche) and Ye Crown (Hen. Mould). There was just one in the Market Place, Man in ye Moon (Widow Hodson), and in what was known as Half (Haff) Street, (today Lichfield Street) stood Ye Dog. Horninglow Street had two pubs, ye Lamb and Flag (J. Clay) and Roebuck (R. Titterton), and finally on Fleet Street corner, the Hoop and Adze. There were the old coaching inns too, such as the George, the Three Queens and the Crown.

Since then the town centre has changed out of recognition, with the recent addition of pedestrianization and shopping precincts. The hustle and bustle around Station Street and High Street is a thing of the past and the number of dwellings in the town has reduced enormously. It is no wonder that the need for town centre pubs has diminished.

High Street

Not only were there plenty of pubs in the High Street but there were at least six breweries too, like the Burton Brewery Co. near the Bargates, T. Salts & Co. next door followed further along by S. Allsopp & Sons. There was J. Yeomans brewery too and, of course, Bass and Worthington. For over two centuries, Burton High Street was home to Bass. Its main offices were situated alongside its famous old brewery with its classically designed brewing plant, traditional brewing processes and the famous Burton Union Fermentation System. Like many town centre thoroughfares, in Burton there was a brewery railway crossing, this one adjacent to one of the street's oldest and best-known pubs, the Blue Posts Inn.

In 1818, there were nine licensed premises in High Street. They were the Old Crown Inn, Blue Posts Inn, Boot Inn, Lamb Inn, White Horse and the Star Inn (possibly once known as Star of Bethlehem). There was also the hotels, Wheatsheaf, White Hart, and the George.

Perhaps the oldest was the Old Crown at No. 15, situated near the present-day Lloyds TSB bank. Like many pubs at the time, it had its own brewery owned by Benjamin Hicklin. There was also the Blue Stoops, run by John Walker around 1739. It was here that the breweries of Benjamin Wilson and Henry Evans began, which later amalgamated with Worthington's. Back in 1766, the original lease for the Blue Posts (also known as the Blue Stumps), was granted by the Earl of Uxbridge to Thomas Hanson. Later the old hostelry became John Yeoman's house. Marstons acquired it and it remained a prestigious part of their estate until September 1925 when it was purchased by Worthington & Co. Ltd. Two years later, they had it demolished and replaced with the one we see today.

Allsopp's brewery in High Street. They had another brewery in Station Street and, of course, later merged with Ind Coope.

Thomas Salt's brewery in High Street. They were later taken over by Bass who acquired their pub estate and closed the brewery.

The Blue Posts in High Street. The name derives from the posts often placed in front of pubs to prevent carts passing over property frontage. In the eighteenth century it was common for innkeepers to paint them blue to identify the beerhouse. The pub has recently been painted green!

Although Bass and Worthington eventually merged, for many years a large Worthington sign on the side of the building has been evidence of the pub's allegiance.

The George, a coaching house in competition with the Three Queens, was described by Underhill as 'a hive of industry where the daily arrival of the mail coaches became a feature of the daily life of the town'. When it went up for sale in 1839, the advertisement pointed out that with the inn went two pews in the Burton parish church. The Town Commissioners, an early version of the Town Council, used to meet there before adjourning to the Angel in the Pig Nook. Owned by Salt's Brewery, it was described as 'a rendezvous for country people, popular on high days and holidays, fair days and Statues Day', but it became less popular with the coming of the railways and the town's expansion. It was replaced by Dewhurst the butcher and today Bird's confectionery shop stands there.

In 1818 the landlord at the Boot Inn, situated near the Bargates at numbers 108-109 High Street, was a John Pemberton and across the road at No. 90 was the Lamb Inn, a William Simnett was mine host there, succeeded by William Millward who ran the pub for around thirty years. Later, on the site of the Lamb, which had been owned by the Burton Brewery Co., were the premises of W.W. Beale & Son, the corn merchants. Much further along, on the corner with Station Street, stood the Wheatsheaf Hotel, run by a Richard Roe and, for many years, a James Eadie house. Across the road at No. 158, was the White Horse, part of the Salt's estate. When that was demolished, the Market Hotel was built on the same site and opened in 1891. A solicitor's office stands there today.

Above: The Philadelphia on the corner of Station Street and High Street. Judging by the numerous pieces of advertising it seems that Bindley & Co.'s Gold Medal ales may have been available!

Below: The High Street in 1962. A rear entrance to the Dog and Partridge in New Street can be seen next to Sleigh's shop. Further along in Bank Square is the Bass sign on the White Lion.

The now-demolished Corporation Arms in New Street back in 1968. On the wasteland to the left once stood a pub called the King of Prussia.

Later, the Coach and Horses opened. Situated at 84 High Street, for many years it was owned by Salt's Brewery. After closure and demolition, offices for Estate Agent, John German, were built on the site. Others, like the Albion Vaults and the Seven Stars, followed. The Albion, at Nos 32-34, close to Darley's bookshop, was part of Bowler's estate and later had the distinction of being the only Everard's house in Burton, bought at an auction sale for £10,300 in 1935. It eventually became the premises of Allandale Machin, the Estate Agents.

Around 1830, three beerhouses, the Cross Keys, Dusty Miller and the Masons Arms, and pubs such as the Dog, opened in High Street. They all lasted for a relatively short period of time. There was the Freehold Tavern and, on the corner with Station Street, the Philadelphia, owned by Bindley's and eventually demolished. The old Martin's bank was situated there later. In 1860, at No. 40 High Street, stood a pub called the Oddfellows Arms. The landlord was Samuel Teat, but it doesn't seem to have survived for long.

By 1960, there were just five licensed premises in High Street. The White Hart and the Blue Posts had survived, along with the Market Hotel and the Albion Vaults. The fifth was a Worthington house, the Golden Eagle, where the Boot Inn originally stood. It was owned by Pegg's Bridge Street brewery and later Nunneley's. Demolished before the construction of the Bargates shopping centre, it is debatable who was more famous at the Golden Eagle, Mr Eric Hardy the landlord, or his monkey.

There are still five licensed premises in High Street, but only the Blue Posts remains from the early days. The other four are much newer. There's the popular Lord Burton, a typical Wetherspoon's outlet standing where Woolworths used to be, with Yates's next door. The Corner House, formerly Peggy's Bar, is there, and a bar restaurant called The Lounge.

Right: The White Hart Hotel in High Street was one of six commercial hotels in the town in the early twentieth century. Run in conjunction with a motor-repair business, it is described here as the most comfortable and up-to-date hotel in the Midlands. The other hotels in Burton then were the George, also in High Street, the Bell Hotel in Horninglow Street, the Station, the Midland and, of course, the Queens.

Below: It was a sad day when the landlord at the Golden Eagle in High Street pulled the last pint. For many years the landlord was Eric Hardy who kept a monkey and a parrot, much to the amusement of his regulars. In this photograph, taken from the Bargates corner in 1963, the pub sign was promoting Worthington E, one of the town's favourite beers at the time.

Above: Peggy's Bar in High Street celebrates its fifth anniversary.

Opposite above: The Corner House, 2004.

Opposite below: The Lord Burton in High Street is on the site of the old Woolworths store. This photograph, taken a few years ago, was in connection with the Burton Civic Society awards.

There is nothing new about the name of a pub being changed. Sometimes it's a straightforward name change, often on change of ownership. At the other extreme, a completely different sort of licensed premises could be built on the site of a previous one which has been demolished, like No. 152 High Street. For many years the Star stood on this site along with its own brewery, the licence being held first by Robert and then Sarah Measom. Another licensee, Mr Gill, was also known by his stage name, Vincente Erne. He was a one-time understudy to George Robey and once toured with Gracie Fields. Later, the Star became part of the Worthington estate and, after being demolished, was replaced by the Galaxy, which had the dubious distinction of being the only Ind Coope pub in town not to sell cask-conditioned ales. Later the Galaxy became the Beehive, followed by Barnaby's and then Café Mocha, until it was relaunched earlier this year as The Lounge. That's six different licensed premises on the one site.

Left: The Star in High Street. Thought to have been called the Star of Bethlehem for a while, it was later replaced by the Galaxy, followed by the Beehive, Barnaby's, Café Mocha and now The Lounge.

Opposite above: The Galaxy in High Street in 1984.

Opposite below: The Galaxy then became Barnaby's.

Having changed from Barnaby's, the High Street building is as Café Mocha before it underwent yet another facelift and reopened as The Lounge.

The Lounge, the sixth licensed premises on the site.

The White Lion in Bank Square in the mid-1960s. It was demolished to make way for the entrance to Coopers Square shopping precinct.

Market Place and Bank Square

As seen above, some of the most interesting public houses in Burton have been situated in the Market Place and across the road in Bank Square. There have been seven altogether. Today there are just two licensed premises, the strangely named Pickled Gherkin, a café bar, and the Old Royal Oak, one of the town's most ancient hostelries, the prefix 'old' being added recently. Originally, the building was a prison and legend has it that only when it ran out of prisoners was it decided to turn it into a pub. For almost three centuries it was called the Royal Oak. A Bass house, it later transferred across to Ind Coope. Then it became Duffey's for a short while before reverting to something close to its original name. As for others – like the Drum and Monkey and the Man in the Moon – all are long gone as, of course, is the Old Bowling Green Inn. Charles Underhill describes it as 'a relic of the old Benedictine Abbey buildings... a building of some dignity and beauty, to which many Burtonians resorted'. In March 1735, an advertisement appeared in the *Derby Mercury* for 'an Inn in the Market Place, Burton, the Bowling Green, including profits from the gaol and the toll of the market'. Eventually it was thought necessary to build a market hall and so, in 1883, the Bowling Green was demolished and the red-brick Market Hall took its place. Another pub close by was the Elephant and Castle. By 1880, it was called the Market Inn and it was in this pub, owned by Nunneley's, that colliers used to gather for a meal of beefsteak and peas. That was until 1909, when it closed altogether.

ROYAL OAK

Opposite: The Royal Oak in the Market Place, one of the oldest pubs in Burton, was originally a prison. For a short while it became known as Duffey's before reverting to its original name – almost.

Right: The Old Royal Oak in the Market Place as it is today.

Below: Burton Market Place dominated by the old Town Hall. The Elephant and Castle can be seen on the right close to the Royal Oak. On the left is the Man in the Moon.

BURTON OLD TOWN HALL,
Market Place
Erected 1772
Pulled down 1883.

Just off Bank Square in 1965. The solicitor's office is thought to be the site of the famous Angel public house.

Opposite the Market Place on Bank Square (originally known as Marketstede and dating back to the early nineteenth century) stood the White Lion, which was demolished in 1967 before work started on the Coopers Square shopping centre. Nearby was the Angel, in what used to be known as the Swine Market or the Pig Nook where pigs were sold from enclosed pens. That area appears to have been an important commercial centre for the town in the Middle Ages. For sixty-one years from 1791-1852, the tenants there were a family named Whitehead. Thomas Whitehead was the landlord for most of that time until Mr Atterbury arrived from the Royal Oak in the Market Place. The magistrates court was held in the pub prior to the police station being built and it was there that the steward of the Marquess of Anglesey received rents and the landlord provided the annual dinner in the old town hall which stood in the Market Place. Close by was the original Evershed's Brewery.

Bond End

Back in 1818, Bond End was regarded as being in the town centre. Records show that three public houses were there: the Nags Head, the Punch Bowl, where a Mary Roe was the licensee, and another pub called the Old White Lion, not to be confused with the White Lion in nearby Bank Square. The landlord was Thomas Bell, who continued to run the pub until the middle of the nineteenth century, by which time it was listed as being in Lichfield Street. Later, the Punch Bowl was run for a period of twenty-four years by Amos Bateman whose father, also called Amos, kept the Forest Gate in Moor Street. Bindley's brewery decided to build a new pub near the original Punch Bowl, which had been owned by J. Marston & Co., and gave it the same name. Over a hundred years later it became known as the Appleby, then Cameo's before becoming the Appleby again.

The Anglesey Arms was in Abbey Street. Dating to the early nineteenth century, it was later known as the Marquis of Anglesey and was owned by Charrington & Co. for a number of years. There was also the Abbey Inn, situated in what is now Manor Drive. Steeped in history, it was here that the Benedictine monks started brewing beer in Burton. There were two public houses in nearby Fleet Street, the ancient Hoop and Adze and the Wheel Inn, both owned by Sydney Evershed's brewery. In 1911, the license for the Hoop and Adze, by then a Marstons' house, was surrendered. The premises were sold ten years later. The name was linked to the coopers' craft, the adze being a tool used by coopers. When Marstons bought the pub, it came with nine cottages, one of which had previously been the Wheel Inn.

The Appleby in Green Street opposite the Ferry Bridge was originally called the Old Punch Bowl. It was extensively modernised in 1984 and reopened as a 'fun pub'. Later it became Cameo's before reverting to the Appleby again.

Lichfield Street

The oldest pub in Lichfield Street is the Dog Inn, which dates back to the beginning of the nineteenth century. A few years later came the Lord Nelson, followed by the Old Spread Eagle. By 1880 there were six hostelries in the street, the Leopard, the Castle Inn and James Eadie's New Inn having been opened by then. Bond End's Old White Lion was recorded as being in Lichfield Street too, but the Lord Nelson which had been bought by Marstons had shut. In 1892, the Castle Inn and the Spread Eagle, both owned by Burton brewer Charles Hill (and then Beard Hill Ltd), were sold along with his brewery in Lichfield Street at an auction which took place at the Queens Hotel. Marston, Thompson and Evershed bought the two pubs. In 1901 the Old White Lion was also purchased by Marstons and closed a few years later. By then, the Spread Eagle had been de-licensed and merged with the Castle Inn next door, which continued as a public house until 1931 when Marstons sold it. Today the Dog Inn and the Leopard are the only pubs left in Lichfield Street, the Dog having reverted to its original name after a few years as an Irish theme pub called O'Neill's.

Above: The Leopard Inn was originally part of Charrington's Brewery, which was situated along Lichfield Street on the site now occupied by B&Q and other modern stores. A London-based company, Charrington United Breweries merged with Bass M&B in the 1960s to become Bass Charrington. For many years, the Leopard has been a Marstons' house but proof of its Charrington heritage is there, partly hidden behind the Marstons' Ales banner near the roof.

Opposite: The Dog Inn in Lichfield Street before it was re-named O'Neill's when Irish theme pubs became popular. It has now reverted to its original name.

Station Street

Altogether there have been thirteen licensed premises in Station Street, which was known as Cat Street until 1835. For many years, the town's two largest breweries were situated here. Although built as long ago as 1863, the Bass Brewery was still referred to as the company's 'new' brewery right up to the time it closed and was replaced with a modern production plant situated nearby. Certainly it was newer than its sister plant in High Street. The other brewery in Station Street belonging to Ind Coope & Allsopp later became known as Allied Breweries' Burton brewery and then Carlsberg Tetley. Much more recently came the amalgamation of Carlsberg Tetley Brewery with the Bass plant next door. Now part of the American brewer, Coors, the combined operation is one of the largest in Europe.

As in much of the town centre, the enormous reduction in the number of people living there goes a long way towards explaining why so many pubs have closed. Even fifty years ago, Station Street had a totally different character and appearance to the one we see today after the loss of virtually all the private houses, including the row of old Bass cottages which have been demolished.

The street's two oldest licensed premises are the Midland Hotel and the Devonshire Arms, both dating back to the middle of the nineteenth century. The Midland, which was bought by Burton brewer James Eadie in 1913 for £1,200, later became a Bass hotel when they took over Eadie's in 1933. By 1880, there were eight pubs in Station Street. The Devonshire had been joined by the Rainbow and Dove, Barrel Inn, Nelson Inn, Staffordshire Knot (originally a Salt's house, later Bass) and, situated near the railway station, the Stanhope Arms. The tenant of the Stanhope Arms was an old retainer of the well-known Stanhope family. There was Bass's New Inn and the Roebuck too and by then the Wheatsheaf Hotel on the corner with High Street was listed as being in Station Street.

The first to disappear were the Rainbow and Dove and the Nelson, the latter a Bindley's pub. The Barrel, at 183 Station Street next to the old Horne Thompson radio and television shop, became the Mayors Arms, part of the Worthington estate, and as late as 1960 was one of just five pubs and a hotel left; the Stanhope Arms having gone along with the Wheatsheaf Hotel. Sadly, since then, that popular Bass house, the Staffordshire Knot, has been demolished and the New Inn at No. 37 near Ellis' tailors shop has closed along with the Mayors Arms.

Six licensed premises remain today but only two of them, the Devonshire and the Roebuck, are what might be termed traditional pubs. In 1956, the Roebuck was rebuilt, and the new building was pushed back around 20ft by sacrificing the public bar of the original house, part of an overdue widening of Station Street. The Devonshire was an Eadie's house before becoming part of the Bass estate when they took over the Eadie's business, including their brewery in Cross Street. Eventually the 'Devvy' became an Ind Coope pub as part of the 1978 swapping arrangements before it was taken over by the Burton Bridge Brewery. The old Midland Hotel is now the Grail Court and there's also Edwards, originally the Locomotive, which was built in 1961 following the closure of the nearby New Inn and the transfer of its license. Nearby are two bar restaurants, the Barracuda Bar (formerly the Gravity and T.P. Woods) and the Dial, situated on the site of a former jeweller's shop famous for its overhanging clock.

Station Street with a tram advertising Bindley's, one of the many small breweries operating in the town at the time.

Station Street around 1960 with Martin's Bank on the corner, the site of the old Philadelphia.

THE DEVONSHIRE ARMS HOTEL,
FAMILY & COMMERCIAL,
Station Street, BURTON-ON-TRENT.

EXCELLENT CUISINE & CELLAR.
Electric Light.   -:-   Moderate Charges.

AN ORDINARY is held every day at an inclusive
charge of 1/-

SAMPLE MENU.

SOUP.	JOINT.
Ox-Tail.	Roast Leg of Mutton.
FISH.	SWEETS.
Filleted Soles.	Apple Tart.
Cheese and Butter.	

Above: Many pubs in Station Street have been demolished, including the Staffordshire Knot. It looks as if it had seen better days when this photograph was taken.

Left: The Devonshire Arms in Station Street was owned by Eadie's Cross Street brewery in the early part of the twentieth century. Rather an appetising menu for a shilling (5p). Later it became an Ind Coope house, before moving across to Bass during the time of the pub swaps and is now one of four hostelries in the town owned by the Burton Bridge Brewery.

Opposite below: In this photograph of Station Street, taken from the Station Bridge, the Roebuck can be seen in the foreground on the right. Situated within a stone's throw of the old Ind Coope brewery, it was often regarded as their brewery tap.

Above: The landlady and her staff are seen here at the Devonshire Arm preparing to welcome their customers.

'I'm going down the Loco' was a common cry back in the 1960s. Opened on 8 November 1962 by Burton MP John Jennings, the Locomotive Inn in Station Street soon became a very popular pub with youngsters. A Bass Worthington house situated adjoining a disused railway crossing, its theme was based on the steam locomotives owned by Bass Ratcliff and Gretton and Worthington & Co. Inside were the Pullman Lounge and the Footplate Bar and there was a grill on the first floor.

The Locomotive subsequently became Edwards.

Midland Hotel,
STATION STREET,
❀ **BURTON - ON - TRENT.** ❀

FIRST-CLASS FAMILY AND COMMERCIAL.

3 Minutes from Railway Station.

The Reception, Billiard, and Private Sitting
Rooms, are electrically lighted, and the house is
replete with comfort.

MOTOR GARAGE. - STABLING.

Excellent Cuisine and Cellar.

TELEPHONE 0723.

Miss CHAMBERLAIN, - - *Manageress.*

Left: An early photograph of the Midland
Hotel on the corner of Station Street and
Guild Street. Electric lights, a billiard room
and stabling were amongst the facilities
available to customers. The hotel is now
called the Grail Court.

Below: The Grail Court Hotel, for many years
the Midland Hotel.

New Street

New Street used to be a far more important thoroughfare than it is today, so perhaps it's not surprising that there have been so many pubs there. In 1818 there were six including the Anchor, one of the town's oldest hostelries. Incorporating its own brewery, Joseph Bowler's, it was later purchased by Marstons in 1891. The Carpenters Arms, situated a little further down from the Anchor, was owned by the nearby Bindley's brewery. Earlier, the Carpenters Arms had its own brewery, owned and run by William Gretton. Virtually next door was the Old Queen's Head with another pub, the King of Prussia, across the road. Also on New Street was the New Wheatsheaf and the Old Eagle. Back in 1579 it seems that an inn called the Bulls Head stood near the corner of New Street and High Street, almost opposite what was called the Abbey Gateway. William Beddoes was the licensee then and much later, in the middle of the eighteenth century, Henry James, described as a bucklemaker, brewer and maltster, lived there. It was rented by Michael Bass in the early nineteenth century and later became a shop. By 1834, there was another pub in New Street called the Spread Eagle, which seems to have closed around 1870.

Left: The corner of New Street and High Street in 1965. The Dog and Partridge can be clearly seen and further along is the Corporation Arms.

Opposite: The signal box in this photograph of New Street taken in 1962 marks the site of a pub called the King of Prussia. Nearby is the Corporation Arms.

Only the Anchor survives. In September 1880, the license for the King of Prussia was transferred to a new premises called the Corporation Arms, a Sydney Evershed house, later Marstons'. They surrendered it on closure in 1970 and the premises were sold in 1973. Another pub in New Street, the Union Inn, was originally called the New Inn. For many years, an Eadie's house, then Bass, the Union is still in business. Like many pubs in Burton, it was part of the estate of the Marquis of Anglesey until, in 1879, it was sold to Bowler's brewery. Later it was leased to Eadie's, who were then taken over by Bass. The Beehive and the Britannia are long gone but many will remember the popular Dog and Partridge which stood on the corner of New Street and Lichfield Street where Littlewoods store is today. With its rear entrance from High Street, for years it was an Eadie's house until it became part of the Bass estate. Two with strange names, the Plum Pudding and the Fish and Quart (another Bindley's house) have disappeared as well. The latter, which stood at 111 New Street, near the hospital, may have had connections with the Burton Abbey. From there, the monks are reputed to have given 300 loaves, 600 herrings and 200 gallons of beer from the monks' kitchen to the poor of the town each year on the anniversary day of the founder. Lost too are the Foundry Inn, another Bindley's pub, situated next to the brewery itself and, close by, the Corporation Arms. Also in New Street was the Crown Inn, originally owned by Thomas Robinson's brewery (a crown can still be seen on the front of the premises) and situated a little further along was the Hare and Hounds and the Green Man, another Bass pub close to what was the Burton Working Mens Club. Around 1860, the Green Man had its own brewery. Also in New Street, the Millwrights Arms, owned by Bindley's and, for a while, by James Porter whose brewery was in Dale Street. The Millwrights, situated next to the fire station, had previously been called the Wheelwrights Arms. On the site today and in stark contrast to the old pub stands a licensed premises called BAR XV. Nearby is Billy's, on the site of which in 1984, was a fun pub called Just William.

NEW STREET, BURTON-ON-TRENT, DURING FLOOD OF 1875

W. B. DARLEY, BURTON-ON-TRENT.

Above: Flood waters in New Street in 1875. The Crown Inn can clearly be seen on the right.

Opposite: The Foundry Inn in New Street was owned by Bindley & Co. Their brewery premises is off the left of the photograph, which was taken in 1900. The landlord was Charles Chapman. His son Albert, pictured standing between his sisters, was later employed by Marstons as a coachbuilder.

Bridge Street

For its comparatively small size, Bridge Street has had a surprisingly large number of licensed premises, as well as a brewery, Nunneley's, which later merged with Marstons. The Three Queens Hotel had its first licence granted back in 1531. Two of the sovereigns who it is claimed enjoyed its hospitality were Mary Queen of Scots on her fateful journey from Chartley Castle to Fotheringay, where she went on trial on a charge of plotting against the Queen's life before being executed, and Adelaide, the consort of William IV, who was also a guest when travelling to Sudbury Hall on a visit to Lord Vernon.

In the old coaching days, the post was collected daily from the Queens and, for many years, a coachman's coat, hat and horn hung in the vestibule. For centuries it was known as the Queens Hotel, before returning to its original name in January 2004. Next door was Bass's Saracen's Head. Once kept by a man called Terry, who had taken part in the Charge of the Light Brigade at Balaclava, it was eventually merged with the Queens. There was the Ship Inn too, a pub built on the site of a chapel erected at the end of the old Burton Bridge by King Edward II to celebrate his victory over Thomas of Lancaster in 1321. The chapel stood until 1771 when the Ship took its place, with a Charles Powis being granted the first licence. There was also the Rose and Crown where William Chambers was the landlord in 1834, the Spirit Vaults, as well as the Plough Inn, which was originally recorded as being at Bridge End. Then there was the famous Fox and Goose, for many years a Bass house until being taken over in 1982 by the adjacent Burton Bridge Brewery and becoming the Bridge Brewery Inn.

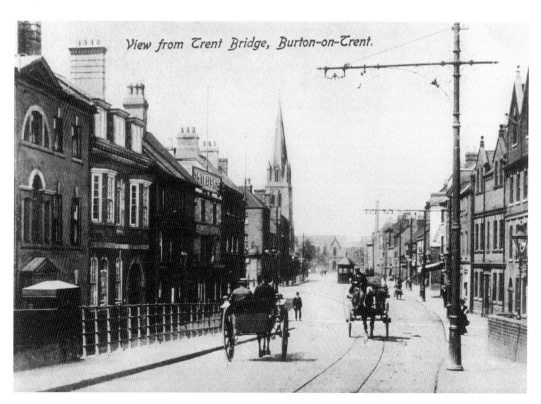

View from Trent Bridge, Burton-on-Trent.

Above: A large crowd has gathered in Bridge Street to watch a procession moving towards the Burton Bridge. The Queens Hotel is on the left, complete with its canopy.

Right: Burton has three micro breweries. The first was the Burton Bridge Brewery, pictured here in its early days.

Opposite: For such a short thoroughfare, Bridge Street had a large number of pubs.

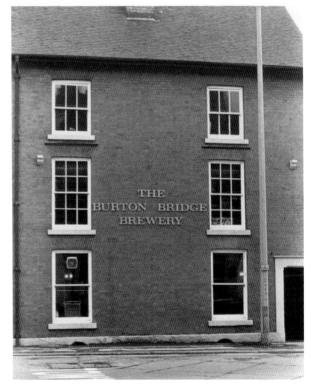

Perhaps the most dramatic changes in Burton have taken place in Horninglow Street. In 1818 there were eight pubs there including the Roebuck Vaults, later the Roebuck Hotel, on the corner with Wetmore Road. There is no mention of it again until 1881 when it was run by Edward Simnett and it seems that it may have become known as Simnett's Vaults for a while. The Talbot Inn too was in Horninglow Street. For many years, it was a house owned by brewers John Thompson & Son of Horninglow and was situated just a few yards away from the Bear Inn where Thompson's had begun brewing back in 1765. The others were the Vine, the Bell Hotel and the Sun, all close together nearby, along with the Three Tuns, although the Fox and Goose and the Saracens Head in what is now Bridge Street were listed as being in Horninglow Street. Earlier around 1792, it seems that there was a pub at No. 5 Horninglow Street called the Lamb and Flag. Situated near the corner with High Street, it was occupied by a family called Clay who apparently brewed there. Later they built what was described as a 'fine house' on the site which Joseph Clay and his son Henry later turned into a bank.

Another pub, the Shoulder of Mutton, run in the 1830s by John Evans, was recorded at different times as being in Horninglow Street and Anderstaff Lane – presumably it must have been close to the corner, possibly where the Roebuck stood. By 1880 it had gone, along with the Three Tuns and the Vine, the latter with its stabling and other

Bass's Roebuck on the corner of Horninglow Street and Wetmore Road.

associated amenities closing around 1840 and later becoming the vicarage for Holy Trinity church. Taking their place were four more pubs, the Plough Inn just down the road from Bass's Rising Sun and, on the other side of Horninglow Street at No. 48, the Beehive, owned by Marstons, as well as the Union Inn on the corner of Brook Street. Further along was another Marstons' house, the Waggoners Arms. The Maltsters Arms, owned by John Thompson & Sons and situated at No. 17 near the corner with Guild Street, was open for a short while around the turn of the century, its licence being surrendered in 1909. The premises later became the Wild Goose café next to Goodhead's, the butcher. The Bell Hotel, owned for years by Samuel Allsopp & Sons, closed in 1912 and, for a while, became the local headquarters of the Territorial Force. By 1960 just three were left: the Waggoners Inn, Roebuck Inn and the long-winded Union Inn and Railway Tavern where two separate houses, Bass's Union Inn and the Railway Tavern just round the corner in Brook Street, had been knocked into one. Today there are no pubs left in Horninglow Street, the Waggoners being the last one to close. The old Bear Inn is an estate agents office, the Talbot, which was next door is an Indian restaurant, and the Plough, a Bass pub, is now a private house. A feature of the Roebuck was its bricked-up windows, a relic of the days of window tax, which was levied on the number of windows in a property in excess of six. Three windows, one above another, facing Wetmore Road were bricked up in this particular premises, which is now a pharmacy.

The building in this photograph, which was taken in 1980, was originally the Beehive Inn situated in Horninglow Street.

Above: What might be described as an early twentieth-century version of a minibus parked outside the Bell Hotel in Horninglow Street. There were six commercial hotels in Burton at the time.

Opposite above: Now demolished, the Waggoners Inn, a Martson's house, was one of many popular pubs in Horninglow Street. Today, none are left.

Opposite below: The design of the doorway confirms that this was the old Bell Hotel in Horninglow Street.

Union Street and Guild Street

Compared with many other parts of the town centre, there have been relatively few public houses in Union Street and Guild Street. In Union Street just one remains, the Burton Union, originally a Sydney Evershed house until they were taken over by Marstons. Bass's Yorkshire Arms has long been demolished and the land on which it stood is now part of Sainsbury's car park. It seems there was a pub called the Fish Inn around 1871. This was run by John Simnett. There was a brewery in Union Street too, that of Thomas Robinson & Co. Today there no pubs at all in Guild Street following the demise of the Seven Stars, owned at the turn of the twentieth century by John Thompson & Sons, as well as the Shakespeare Inn and, more recently, the Guild Tavern, a Bass house.

Above: Marstons' Burton Union is the only pub in Union Street today.

Right: The former Mayors Arms in Station Street has now been demolished to make way for Worthington Way.

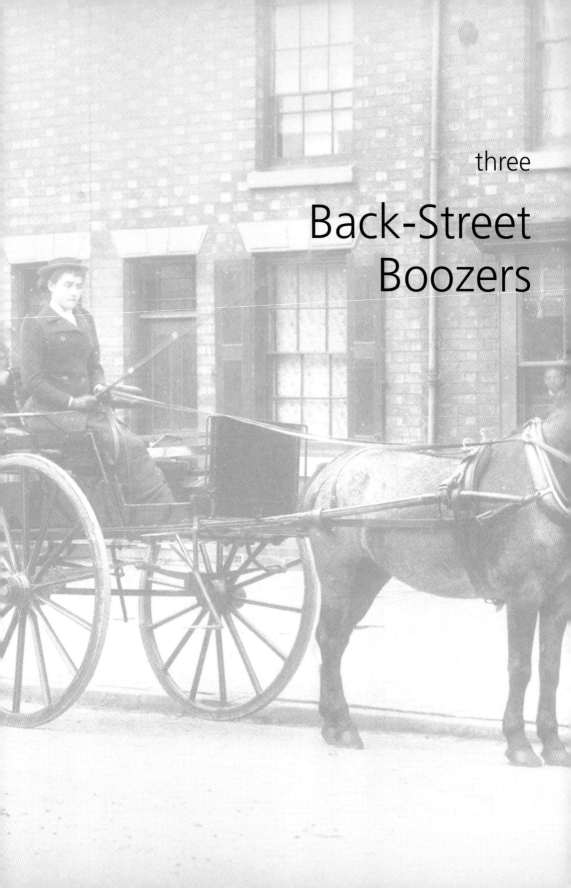

three

Back-Street
Boozers

Read any publication about public houses and you can be fairly certain that there will be a section on back-street boozers. So why should this one be any different? It's not a derogatory term, rather an authentic description of an enormous number of pubs which have usually provided good ale and cheerful company over numerous years. Although many of the pubs which have closed in Burton were old-fashioned boozers, often on street corners, the town still has its fair share, although some have struggled to survive. Sadly they often had difficulty in attracting young customers.

Back in 1834 there were five public houses recorded as being in Anderstaff Lane, as it was called until the middle of the nineteenth century when it became known as Wetmore Road. They were the Shoulder of Mutton and the Swan, plus three beerhouses, the Dragoon, the Malt Shovel – for many years a Worthington pub – and the Old Peacock. Later, towards the end of the nineteenth century after the name of the road changed, another four pubs were built, the Coopers Arms, owned for many years by the Burton Brewery Co. and situated close to the Swan, as well as the Brewers Arms further along. There was the Masons Arms too, a Marstons' house which finished trading in 1909, and John Thompson's Crown and Anchor. A little later, another John Thompson pub, the Great Northern Inn, opened. In 1935, the Crown and Anchor was demolished and a new pub was built on the same site and given the same name.

This photograph was taken outside the Prince Alfred Inn in Derby Street. As well as serving ales, porter, wines, spirits, liquor and tobacco, it appears that Mark King, the licensee, also had a pony and trap for hire.

A small crowd has gathered outside the Great Northern Inn in Wetmore Road following what appears to be some sort of traffic accident. The date is thought to be around 1925. A vehicle from Machin's Garage is in attendance and a policeman seems to have things under control.

The Cricketers Arms in Meadow Lane was the only Burton pub built on an island. Here, pictured with an Allsopp's sign, it is a reminder that there is nothing new about lager brewing in Burton. The pub's name is derived from its proximity to the cricket grounds of Burton Gentlemen and Bass. This picture was taken after the license had passed from Mr Oldham to his widow, Emma. Another licensee was Eric Hardy, who also kept the Roebuck in Station Street and the Golden Eagle in High Street with the assistance of his menagerie.

By 1960, just four pubs were left: the Great Northern, Coopers, Malt Shovel and the Crown and Anchor which exists today with the Great Northern, owned by the Burton Bridge Brewery. Nearby in Meadow Road off the Burton Bridge stood the Cricketers Arms close to the old Whitehead's brewery. Later Boddington's and Everard's brewed there.

There were four pubs in nearby Hawkins Lane in 1880: the London and North Western, Dixie Inn, Tiger Inn, for years an Allsopp's house, and the Mount Pleasant which, although a Salt's pub, was owned for a while by the Great Northern Railway Co. The London and North Western belonged to a railway company of the same name, although it became a Worthington house later. The Shoulder of Mutton was built a little later and survived for a relatively short period of time. By 1960, only the Dixie was left. The Tiger, further along, had become a general store; the Mount Pleasant, a private house; and on the site of the London and North Western stood the premises of J. Burman & Sons' cooperage. Since then, the Dixie has closed so there are no pubs left in Hawkins Lane today.

In the mid-nineteenth century, the Black Horse was the only pub in Moor Street and it still survives. A Sydney Evershed house for many years, the licensee was Frank Ralley, who took over from Harley Clarke in 1912. The pub was run by members of the same family for the next forty years, Charlotte Ralley taking over the tenancy on her husband's death in 1925. Eighteen years later, their daughter Faith (Doll) Hudson and her husband Bill were tenants until 1952. Faith, now ninety-four, lives in Winshill. Later the Robin Hood opened in Moor Street. It lasted a comparatively short period of time. There was the Forest Gate too which was a beerhouse owned by John Thompson & Sons. After eighty years as Marstons' pub, it closed and the premises were converted into a flower shop called the Florist Gate! Another Moor Street pub, the Warwick Arms, has also closed, but the Builders Arms, re-titled Mulligan's for a short time, has survived after returning to its original name.

The only two pubs in Orchard Street have both closed. One, the Woolpack, was a Nunneley's house and the other, the Orchard Inn, was originally a Thompson & Sons pub

Did the Dixie belong to Ind Coope or was it an Ansell's house when this photograph was taken in 1984? The answer is both. The Burton brewer had merged with Ansell's of Birmingham to form Allied Breweries. In any case the pub's days were numbered.

Celebrations at Marstons' Black Horse in Moor Street. The landlady at the time was Charlotte Ralley.

The Black Horse
in 2004.

The Forest Gate in Moor Street was built in 1829 on land known as the Goose Moor. The pub was owned by John Thompson & Son before they merged with Marstons. After it closed, the pub became a flower shop called the Florist Gate.

Above: The Builders Arms in Moor Street back in 1984.

Opposite: The day that 'all day drinking' was first allowed in the Coopers Tavern. Here Andrew (Cocky) Myrtle seems determined to make the most of it.

de-licensed and sold in 1938. Also lost are the three houses in Park Street, originally Pinfold Lane, an Eadie's pub the Barley Mow in around 1834; the Red Lion, owned and run by John King; and the Park Inn. There were just two pubs in Paget Street: the Dolphin and Marstons' Dusty Miller, the latter de-licensed in 1923. When the terraced housing in Canal Street was demolished, the Golden Ball went too. It had been one of many in Burton to serve Bass straight from the cask. In nearby Dale Street, home to the old brewery of J. Porter & Son, was the Brickmakers Arms which later disappeared along with almost 100 houses.

Mosley Street has no pubs left either. The Mosley Arms, a Marstons' pub, and Who'd Have Thought It both closed long ago. The Brewers Arms and Sydney Evershed's Rose and Crown, another pub featuring a monkey as an attraction, have shut, along with the Coopers Arms, an Allsopp's house, and the British Crown (situated next to the Roebuck on the corner with Station Street), sold in 1951. In nearby Cross Street, Bass's Alma Hotel with its six-day licence, later renamed the Emerald, continued to trade under that name until destroyed by an explosion. The Vine Inn closed too, leaving the Coopers Tavern, often regarded as the Bass brewery tap, as the last one to survive.

There have been just two pubs in Byrkley Street, the Berkeley Arms and the British Oak, recently bought by the Old Cottage Brewery and renamed the Old Cottage Tavern. As for St Paul's Street East, later King Edward Place, the only pub there, the Lifeboat Inn, became the Railway Inn, a Bass house, before being demolished. There were two in Borough Road as well, the Station Hotel and the Bowling Green. Built around 1833 at the same time as the station bridge itself, the Station Hotel was originally owned by Salt's brewery, before transferring across to Bass when they took over Salt's business in 1927, eventually becoming an Ind Coope house in 1978. After being closed for nearly two years, it was badly damaged by a fire in February 2004.

In Waterloo Street there have been six pubs altogether. Three have closed: the Waterloo Inn, the Duke of Wellington, a Marstons' house which was de-licensed in 1908 and sold four years later, and the Britannia Inn, an old Evershed's pub on the corner of Byrkley Street which is now council offices. The three that remain are the Rams Head, for many years a Worthington house, the Loaf and Cheese and the Trafalgar.

Coopers Tavern in Cross Street is one of the town's most famous pubs, photographed here in its Bass house days. To the astonishment of its regulars, it was sold to Hardy & Hanson of Kimberley.

Above: The Station Hotel was originally owned by Salt's. They were eventually taken over by Bass and the Station continued under their banner until the 1978 pub swaps when it became an Ind Coope house.

Opposite below: It seems that a trusting cyclist has popped into Bass's Loaf and Cheese in Waterloo Street for a swift half.

Above: For some time The Station Hotel has been called The Station. It is all very confusing for the visitors to the town, who sometimes think it is the entrance to the railway station a few yards away. Here on the left of the building, the old Salt's sign has been replaced by an advertisement for Arctic Lite.

Branston Road isn't exactly a back street, but over the years, most of its public houses, nine of them altogether, might be best described as good old-fashioned boozers. There was a Bass house called the George and Dragon, Worthington & Co.'s Waterloo Inn and two White Lion pubs, confusing particularly as they were situated close to each other, near what was known at the time as Uxbridge Road, now Queen Street. Another long-forgotten pub nearby was called the Holly Bush. There was also the Sportsman Inn, a Bindley's house called the Old English Gentleman; and the Welcome Inn, a Beard Hill pub which was also owned for a while by the Midland Railway Co. and situated close to Hill's brewery. Both closed in 1909. Also on Branston Road were the Branston Arms and the Sportsman. These are the only two remaining, the latter being an Eadie's house until it was sold to Charrington's in 1888. They passed it on to Worthington & Co. in 1926.

The Blackpool Inn in Blackpool Street was built in 1897 and is not, as many think, named after the seaside resort. In fact the correct spelling was the Black Pool, after the name of a nearby pond. It was a Charrington pub until 1926 when Charrington & Co. decided to concentrate their business in London and on the 2 and 3 February 1926, eighty-five of their public houses in the Midlands were put up for sale including three in Burton, the Sportsman Inn, the Oddfellows Arms in Uxbridge Street, both of which had full licenses, along with the Blackpool Inn, a beerhouse. At the end of the second day of the sale their Abbey brewery in Lichfield Street was also disposed of along with offices,

Above: The Sportsman in Branston Road.

Opposite above: One of the first pubs in Burton to offer food was the Branston Arms on Branston Road. It was a Bass pub, run at the time by well-known landlord Bill Pumphrey. In the sixties, his chicken-in-the-basket or scampi served with generous portions of chips became very popular. It was just the place to impress your girlfriend!

The Blackpool Inn – nothing to do with the holiday resort. Apparently, back in the sixteenth century, a feud between the monks of Burton Abbey and the peasants of Drakelow resulted in the deaths of two people close to a pond near the River Trent. This became known as the Black Pool. Hence the name the Blackpool Inn situated, of course, in Blackpool Street.

Marstons' New Talbot Hotel back in 1984. It replaced the old Talbot Inn which had stood there since the days when Anglesey Road was called Varlow Street.

maltings and a cooperage, together with two further licensed houses, the Marquis of Anglesey and the Leopard Inn adjoining the brewery.

Part of what is now Anglesey Road was originally known as Varlow Street. On this street, the Talbot Hotel was situated. Later it was demolished and replaced with the New Talbot Hotel which remains today along with the Coopers Arms which was originally in Kimmersitch Street, the old name for the other end of Anglesey Road. When the Coopers was erected in 1905, the licences of two pubs were surrendered and transferred across, they were the old Coopers in Mosley Street and the Seven Stars in Guild Street.

Very few pubs have opened in Burton in the last fifty years. One welcome addition has been the Thomas Sykes on the site of the Heritage Brewery, just off Anglesey Road. Five public houses have been lost from Uxbridge Street: Bass's Earl Grey Inn; the Bull's Head; an Eadie's pub before Bass acquired it; the Cross Keys, which was delicensed and sold in 1931; and the Marquis of Lorne, a Worthington pub for many years, which is now a private house; along with the Talbot Inn which was owned by Chas. Hill's brewery until 1892. Originally a coaching house, the name stemmed from the talbot, a breed of dog which ran in front of the coach. Just two pubs remain in Uxbridge Street, the Oddfellows Arms and the Labourers Union, originally a beerhouse renowned for many years for the excellence of its Worthington ales. One of its main features was a 'gentlemen only' room and there was a long corridor in which many customers preferred to drink. Like many pubs, it had a 'jug and bottle' where beer could be bought for home consumption.

There were two pubs in Wood Street, the long lost Woolpack and the Gladstone Inn, which moved across from the Bass estate to Ind Coope in 1978. The only pub to have traded in All Saints Road, the Argyle Arms, remains. It was originally an Eadie's house.

Above: Marstons' Coopers Arms in Anglesey Road on the corner with Walker Street.

Right: Visitors to the Thomas Sykes situated just off Anglesey Road could be forgiven for thinking they had taken a step back to pre-war days. The traditional-style pub is situated on the site of the now defunct Heritage brewery.

Uxbridge Street. Just two pubs remain in Uxbridge Street, the Oddfellows Arms and the Labourer's Union. Five have been lost.

The Oddfellows Arms in Uxbridge Street was one of five pubs in Burton owned by Charrington & Co. of London. The others were the Leopard, adjacent to the brewery, the Marquis of Anglesey, the Sportsman and the Oddfellows.

Ind Coope's Gladstone Inn in King Street. This was one of the houses transferred from Bass to Ind Coope during the 1978 pub swaps.

Today there are no pubs in Napier Street with the demise of the Blue Stumps (also known as the Blue Posts), a Bass house, later part of Allsopp's estate. More recently, the Napier Arms was situated there. It was owned by the Burton Building Co. before it also became part of the Allsopp's estate. Lost too is James Street's Vulcan Inn which, like some other Burton pubs, was owned for a time by the Midland Railway Co. Also lost was the Sheffield Arms in Sheffield Street, originally a Bindley's house, and the Outwoods Inn in Henry Street, a John Bell & Co.'s pub, one of the less well-known Burton brewers. In Queen Street, the Queens Arms on the corner of King Street is now a private house, but the Uxbridge Arms on the corner of Branston Road, for many years a Bass pub, is still in business.

There were six public houses in Wellington Street. The Highland Laddie, the Blue Ball and the Nelson all disappeared, leaving the Wellington Arms, Compasses, originally a Salt's house, and the Oak and Ivy, all well over 100 years old, remaining. On the new Centrum Business Park is the Bill Brewer, one of the few new pubs to be built in Burton recently.

In Derby Street, there were six public houses including the Railway Bridge Inn on Derby Turn, for many years a James Eadie pub. There was also the Rifleman Inn, owned by Bass; the British Lion on the corner of Victoria Road, originally a Worthington house; and the Rose and Crown, at one time part of the Sydney Evershed estate. There was also the Prince Alfred, an old Eadie's house; the Smithfield Hotel; and a nearby pub, the Boathouse known as Little Burton at the time. The Rifleman is now a bed shop and the British Lion has gone too, along with the Smithfield Hotel which closed in 1960 and later was converted into offices. The Railway Bridge Inn was also demolished. Recently, the Rose and Crown was renamed the Bell and Brewer on change of ownership and the Prince Alfred, originally a Truman's pub and situated across the road from their brewery, is now one of four Burton Bridge Brewery outlets in the town and renamed the Alfred.

Above: Bass Worthington's Argyle Arms on the corner of All Saints Road and Uxbridge Street.

Right: There are no pubs in Napier Street now. This was the Blue Stumps. There was also the Napier Arms, which is now a dress shop.

Opposite above: The Napier Arms, which used to be owned by the Burton Building Co.

Bill Babbington at the Compasses in Wellington Street back in 1993, making the most of a promotion offering five pints for the price of four.

Bass Worthington's Wellington Arms in 1984.

The Bill Brewer is the only new pub to open in Burton recently.

The Railway Bridge Inn at Derby Turn was a popular Bass house. This photograph was taken in 1984.

When this photograph was taken twenty years ago, the pub on the junction of Derby Street and Byrkley Street was called the Rose and Crown and was owned by Courage. One of many pubs in Burton to have its name changed, it is now called the Bell and Brewer.

The Alfred in Derby Street is owned by Burton Bridge Brewery. It was originally called the Prince Alfred, a Truman's house.

There was just one pub in Sydney Street, the Hanbury Arms, situated on the corner with Goodman Street. Originally a Truman's house, it became a John Smith's outlet. There is one pub in Parker Street, the Black Eagle (also known as the Eagle Hotel) but the solitary one in Princess Street, Bass's Admiral Benbow, is now a private house. Around 1879, it seems there may have been a licensed premises in Stafford Street called the Stafford Hotel, run by Henry Stokes. Certainly a licence was applied for in that name, but little is known about it.

Altogether, there have been five pubs in Victoria Street: the Victoria Arms at No. 31, for many years an Allsopp's house; the Essex Arms; the Lord Napier Inn; the Lord Nelson on the corner with Victoria Road; and the Prince of Wales and the Duke of York, owned by Bowler's Anchor Brewery before eventually becoming a Marstons' pub. There was also a hotel called the Victoria at No. 1 on the corner with Albert Street. By early 1960, just three houses remained, the Duke of York, Lord Napier and the Essex Arms, but in July of that year, the Essex closed. Only the Duke of York has survived since. There was a brewery too in Victoria Street, the long-forgotten Scattergood's.

The longest surviving pub in Victoria Crescent was the Shakepeare Inn, originally a James Eadie house. There were three others: the Prince of Wales, owned for a while by Charrington & Co., the Dingo Inn, and the Steam Packet. The Dingo Inn was near Old Cooper's brewery, the pub trading for a short time around 1860, as did the Steam Packet with landlord Abraham Atkins. In Dallow Street, there was the old Star Inn, a Bass pub on the corner with Victoria Crescent dating back to around 1900. It is now a cycle shop.

The Hanbury Arms on the corner of Sydney Street and Goodman Street is seen here advertising the products of John Smith's Tadcaster brewery. At one time, it was rare for beers brewed outside the town to achieve any degree of popularity.

Truman's, the London brewer, was one of many who decided to set up in Burton. The Prince Alfred in Derby Street was one of five pubs they owned in the town.

For many years, one of the best examples of a popular back-street boozer has been the Duke of York, a Marstons' house on the corner of Victoria Street and Edward Street. This photograph, which has hung in the pub for many years, shows the landlord and his wife standing in the doorway.

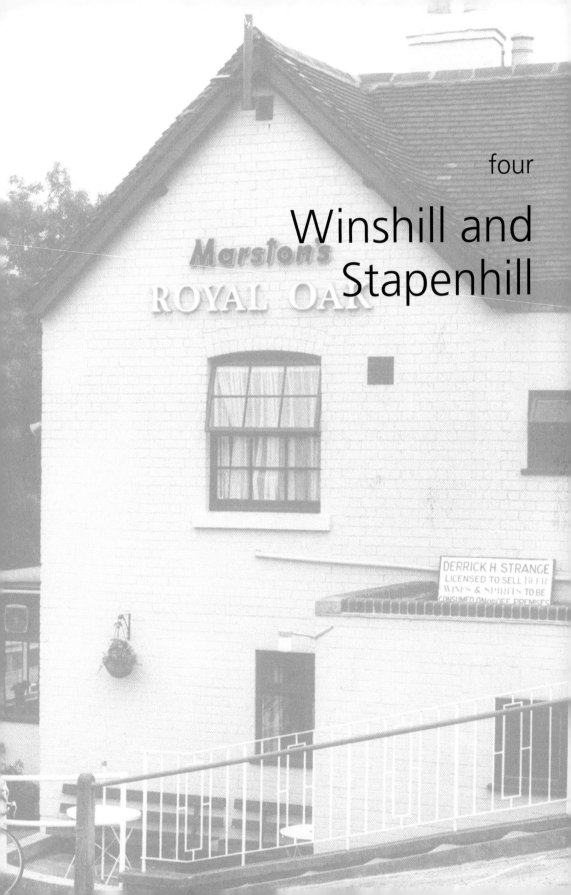

four

Winshill and Stapenhill

The Gardens, *c.* 1950.

Until the late nineteenth century, Winshill and Stapenhill were two villages just 'over the border' into Derbyshire; the boundary between Derbyshire and Staffordshire being the River Trent. Since then, there has been no need for inhabitants of either of those two suburbs of Burton to venture far in search of a decent pint of beer, each has had quite enough pubs to satisfy the needs of the locals without having to cross the river or head towards South Derbyshire. Over the years, there have been almost thirty pubs on the far side of the Trent. Today there are twenty. Although well over half of the pubs in Burton have closed, there are areas where the survival rates have been relatively high. Winshill and Stapenhill are good examples.

The Swan Inn at the bottom of Bearwood Hill Road and Ashby Road has always been rather more than just a licensed premises. Legend has it that its name is derived from the first letters of the villages of Stapenhill, Winshill, Ashby and Newton Solney, each of which can be found by taking one of the roads leading from it. Thanks to an enormous neon Bass sign high up in front of the roof, for generations it was something of a landmark, a constant reminder to everyone crossing the River Trent on the Burton Bridge that the town was home to arguably the most famous brewing company in England. That's until the day no Burtonian thought would ever come, when Hardy & Hanson of Kimberley bought the pub along with four other Bass houses in the area and replaced the famous old sign with a new one informing everyone that Kimberley ales were now available.

If the sign over the door at The Nelson was correct, the pub in Nelson Street had just celebrated its hundredth anniversary when this photograph was taken in the early 1980s.

For decades it was almost unheard of for a Burton pub to sell beers which weren't brewed in the town itself. So imagine the surprise when a famous Bass house like the Swan Inn was sold to Hardy & Hanson of Kimberley along with four other pubs in the area. The sight of an enormous Kimberley neon on the front of the building replacing the famous Bass sign came as something of a shock to Burtonians.

In Winshill, the Sump, formerly called the Royal Oak is, and always has been, the only public house on Newton Road, just as the Waterloo Inn has been the only watering hole on Ashby Road. For many years a Bass house, the Waterloo was owned by Marstons around the turn of the twentieth century. The (Old) Gate Inn at the bottom of Berry Hedge Lane closed before the First World War. With its pleasure gardens and an orchard nearby, it must have been a popular hostelry in its day. It is an attractive cottage now but even though the thatched roof has gone, it is still recognisable as the pub which was captured by various amateur photographers at the turn of the twentieth century. Around 1850, there are records of a pub in old Winshill called the Jolly Farmer where the licensee was a John Plummer, and another called Speed-the-Plough, the landlord there being George Pipes. Little else is known about either of those two houses. Sadly, the Alma Inn, a popular Bass pub on the corner of Hawfield Lane and Church Hill Street, has been demolished and the Queens Arms, originally a Bindley's house before Ind Coope bought it, was the last pub in Winshill to shut. The Nelson Inn, like the Gate, was originally owned by William Pickering before it became an Ind Coope house. It is still up and running. The Anglesey Arms, a Marstons' house on Bearwood Hill Road thrives (that is the address despite the Church Hill Street road sign on the front of the pub), and the Jubilee which opened in 1977 serves the locals in that part of Winshill. Its licence was transferred from the Alma. The aptly named Travellers Rest, originally an Eadie's, then a Bass, pub is handily situated across the road from Winshill church, and is still with us too.

Right: The Royal Oak along Newton Road before it was renamed the Sump. Off the photograph to the left is the historic Greensmith's Mill.

Opposite above: The Waterloo on Ashby Road.

Opposite below: It was before the First World War when the last pints were pulled at the Old Gate Inn at the bottom of Berry Hedge Lane in Winshill. In this picture, the pub sign was fixed to the wall of the inn. The pub was converted into an attractive cottage which can still be seen today.

The Queens Arms, an Ind Coope pub situated in West Street, is now a fish and chip shop.

The Queens has had its chips.

The Anglesey Arms in Winshill as it looked many years ago.

Relatively few pubs have opened in Burton since the war but one that has is the Jubilee in Hawfield Lane, Winshill which started trading in 1977. Here photographed in its time as a Bass house, it later it became a Burtonwood Brewery pub.

In Stapenhill there are older pubs like the Elms Inn, for a short time a Gibbs Mew house after many years selling Bass and Worthington beers. A large painted sign on the front of the pub appears to reaffirm its allegiance to Bass. In fact, it was part of the Worthington estate before Bass and Worthington merged. In Main Street was the original Punch Bowl, along with its pleasure gardens. Back in the 1860s, when a landlord by the name of Thomas Wilson ran the pub owned by Allsopp's, not only were strawberries, teas and refreshments on offer, but also what was known as a quadrille band on some evenings as well as a gymnasium. Later, it was owned by Hill & Co., then Beard Hill. The old Punch Bowl was demolished in the 1930s and replaced by the one we see today and in Ferry Street stands the New Inn, for years a Marstons' house, along with the Gardens Hotel which was originally a Boddington house.

The Plough Inn in Ford Street (formerly Pickering Street) was an Ind Coope pub and, for those who liked to enjoy their beer dispensed straight from the cask, there was the Travellers Rest along Stanton Road, now a private house. Also on Stanton Road, the original Black Horse, a Thompson's pub dating back to the nineteenth century, was demolished and replaced in 1940 by a new one which was given the same name. Over the years, regulars at the Barley Mow have often referred to it as the Barley. That is the official name now for a pub which was owned by Salt's brewery before Bass acquired their estate.

Beer was carried up from the cellar steps straight from the wood at the Crown on Rosliston Road, which was run by different members of the Morris family for over forty years. After being demolished in 1960, it was replaced with a new pub bearing the same name which began as an Ind Coope house before being bought by the Burtonwood Brewery and, in July of the same year, a new Bass pub opened, the Copper Hearth on Stanton Road.

The Travellers Rest in Church Hill Street, Winshill. In the foreground are the pillars at the bottom of the path leading to St Mark's church.

The Punch Bowl in Stapenhill rebuilt in 1930s.

Two years later, a brand new Marstons' house, The Grove on Merridale Road, was in business, not to be confused with the old Grove Hotel which was a grocer's shop before becoming a pub, but is now a hairdresser's salon. There's the Boathouse on the Dingle on the banks of the River Trent and the Dart Inn on Short Street, originally a prefabricated building which opened in October 1951, the licence having been transferred from the Bear Inn, the original application for a licence having been granted to Marstons in early 1940. Initially a complete new public house was to have been built but, owing to the war and problems with building new premises, that was not possible. There was no sleeping accommodation for the licensee, who had to make do with a caravan. Eventually the prefabricated building was replaced by the pub we see today.

When it was a Marstons' pub, the Freehold Tavern on the corner of Rosliston Road and Long Street, which closed a few years ago, may not have had a lot in common with the Queens in Winshill but it has now – both are fish and chip shops. Another public house in Stapenhill in the 1850s was the Brickmakers, situated on the road to Drakelow, and today, on a row of cottages in St Peter's Street, there is an inscription with the words 'the North Pole Inn'. Although there are no records of a licensed premises on this site, it does appear to have been a public house back in the seventeenth century. Apparently an old vicar of Stapenhill, the Revd Clay had the pub closed down because he didn't approve of his parishioners visiting what he called a 'den of iniquity'. The pub, which served beers brewed in Thomas Salt's High Street brewery, was closed down in the early nineteenth century, but the cellars remain, as do the old oak beams and daub and wattle internal walls.

Evidence that the Punch Bowl in Stapenhill was once a Hill & Sons pub.

Above: The Gardens in Stapenhill's Short Street in the early 1980s. An Ind Coope pub, it is one of three pubs in the town with a bowling green.

Opposite: The New Inn in Ferry Street around thirty years ago.

The Travellers Rest, an old Bass house in Stanton Road.

Only a handful of new pubs have been built in Burton in the last fifty years. One of them is the spacious Black Horse, a Marstons' house on Stanton Road. This photograph was taken in the mid–1980s.

Bass's Barley Mow in 1984.

The Barley in 2004. The Barley, in Stapenhill's Main Street, is the new name for the Barley Mow, although regulars have been using the shorter version for many years. Originally a coaching house, it is also reputed to have been the location of the fire brigade for Stapenhill village. A manual fire pump had been there for quite some time. The Barley is one of the few Burton pubs still to have a bowling green.

Bass's Copper Hearth on Stanton Road opened on 25 June 1960.

The new Grove in Stapenhill opened in 1962.

Mind my bike! A thirsty customer has obviously popped into the Grove Hotel in Woods Lane, Stapenhill, for a quick pint leaving his bicycle propped up outside. The building is now used as a hairdresser's shop.

The Boathouse Inn in the Dingle, Stapenhill, in the winter of 1984. The pub is situated on the site of the ferryman's house in the days before the ferry bridge was built. Later, the property was owned by Dobson's the boat builders and the boat sheds stood where the pub is today.

The Dart Inn, Short Street, which replaced the original prefabricated pub.

Marstons' Freehold Tavern in Stapenhill. Like the Queens in Winshill, it is now a fish and chip shop.

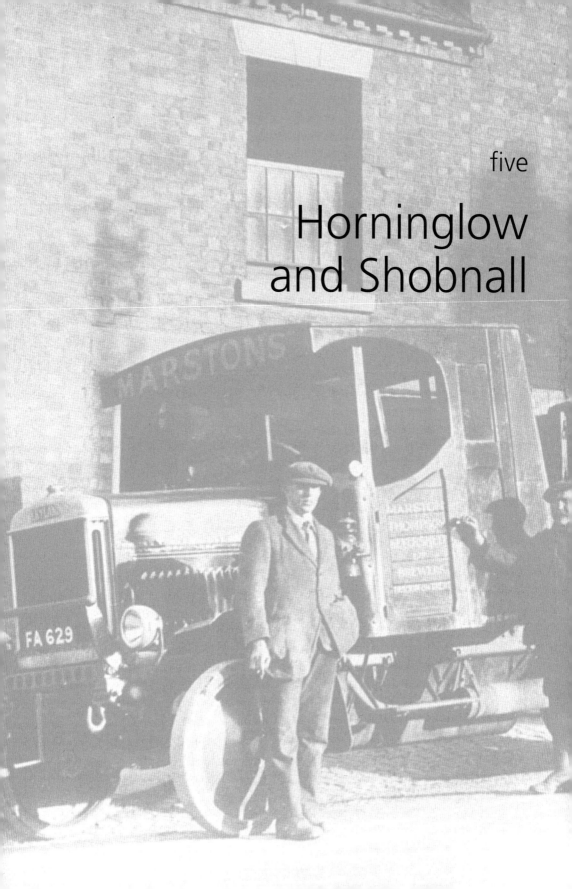

five

Horninglow
and Shobnall

Horninglow Road. The Royal Oak is on the left. Very few pubs have closed along this stretch of road.

In stark contrast to Horninglow Street where there are no pubs remaining, most of those in Horninglow Road and Horninglow Road (North) have survived. That is good news for enthusiastic beer drinkers who continue the old tradition of 'doing the mile'; that's the drag from the top of Horninglow Road (North) as far as Derby Turn.

Until it closed some years ago, they would probably have started with a pint of draught Bass at the Gate Inn on Tutbury Road before moving down Horninglow Road North to sample the Marstons at the Plough Inn. Then down the hill, calling in for a quick pint at the Red Lion before moving on to try the draught Bass (Ind Coope's ale after the 1978 pub swap) at the New Inn. Lottie Wardle was the celebrated landlady at the Foresters Arms, another Bass house. Then on to the Royal Oak, at the corner of Wyggeston Street, an Eadie's pub before the Bass takeover, before moving to the Navigation to sample the Ind Coope product followed by a swift beer at the Crescent Hotel, finishing up at the Victoria Inn.

Surprisingly, of these nine pubs, only the Gate has shut, one of half a dozen pubs to close in Burton since the late 1980s. Those with a greater thirst to quench may have ventured even further into Horninglow Street in the days when there were plenty to choose from there, or maybe into Victoria Crescent, calling in at the Shakespeare, or even as far as Waterloo Street. Alternatively, some could have walked down to the Derby Turn Inn where the original pub was replaced in 1964, finally calling in at the old Derby Inn in Derby Street. These days, for the more energetic, the crawl could begin at the Beacon on Tutbury Road, a few hundred yards away from the old starting point at the Gate. Constructed during the early part of the Second World War when building restrictions came into place in 1940, work on the beacon was only allowed to continue to completion because the structure had reached the stage where the building was above window height. A few years ago, the pub was struck by severe lightning and badly damaged.

The New Inn in Horninglow Road (North) in 1984, an Ind Coope house at this time.

The Plough Inn, the popular Marstons' house at the top of Horninglow Road (North) in 1984. The landlord at this time, John Barrington-Earp, is still pulling pints there today.

The Red Lion is on the corner of Horninglow Road (North) and Rolleston Road and has been a Marstons' pub since the days when their brewery was situated in Horninglow.

For many years, the Foresters Arms in Horninglow Road was known as Lottie Wardell's after the name of its well-known landlady.

The Royal Oak in Horninglow Road (North) has the longest-serving landlord in Burton, having run the same pub for over twenty-one years.

The window cleaner arrives at the Navigation in Horninglow Road during its days as an Ind Coope pub.

Above: Bass's Crescent Hotel in Horninglow Road.

Below: Marstons' Victoria Inn back in 1984.

Above: Bass Worthington's Derby Turn.

Below: A delivery of hogsheads and crates of bottled beer at the Gate Inn on Tutbury Road. In the early part of the twentieth century, the Gate was a Marstons' pub. The landlord, on the left, was Leonard Forbes who later founded Forbes and West, joiners and undertakers. Note the solid tyres on the dray. The driver, on the right, is Albert Wright who later became a foreman in the transport department at Marstons' brewery.

Bass's Gate Inn, not long before de-licensing. It was often the starting point for an evening's stroll, taking in the various pubs along the Horninglow mile.

The Wyggeston Hotel in Calais Road. A popular hostelry, it was one of half a dozen in Burton with a bowling green. This photograph was taken shortly after it had won a Civic Society award.

Architecturally, one of the most impressive pubs in the town is the Wyggeston Hotel on Calais Road named after William Wyggeston of Leicester, a wool merchant who owned a large estate in Horninglow. Built in 1904 and opened on Boxing Day that year, it was originally a Salt's house before passing over to Bass. Sadly its bowling green, which opened in 1906, became a car park sixty-three years later. Apparently one of the hotel's claims to fame was to be chosen by the BBC when they were recording the old radio programme *Down Your Way* with Richard Dimbleby.

There was a quite a contrast between the 'Wyggy' and, arguably, the most unlikely pub in Burton, the Avenue in St John's Road, Horninglow. Being a prefab, rather like the houses built to a similar design just after the war, it was expected to last a relatively short period of time. Over forty years later, 'the shed', as it was often called, was still in business until finally being demolished in September 1990 after a fire. Another pub in Horninglow was the Plough and Horses. Other than being open in 1835 and run by Morris Upton, little more seems to be known about it.

Perhaps the best-known public house in Shobnall was the Mount Pleasant Inn thought to be known originally as the Gateway to Sinai. Although situated on the canal bank, which made it very popular with anglers, the pub almost certainly dates back to a time before the canal was constructed. Often referred to as Bessie Bull's, it closed in 1961 having been in the tenancy of members of the same family for over 100 years. It was also

This is (or rather was) a pub. The Avenue in St John's Road, Horninglow, was a prefab. Designed to last a relatively short period of time, prefabricated buildings, many of which were built just after the war, often lasted for decades. The Avenue, which opened in 1949, finally closed in September 1990 and, after a fire, was subsequently demolished.

The Mount Pleasant cribbage team with their trophies for the 1954/55 season.

popular with hundreds of Burton people taking a favourite stroll alongside the canal where they were always assured of a warm welcome by the landlord who, it was said, kept one of the best pints of ale in town. In stark contrast, much earlier, the Mount Pleasant Inn had become known as the 'blood tub', which might have had something to do with barge men who, it seemed, had the occasional fight there. Although usually thought of as a Marstons' house, like others in that part of Burton, the pub was owned by the Midland Railway Co. who leased it to the brewery and it remained the property of British Railways until it was eventually demolished. Further along Shobnall Road is the Albion Hotel, for many years a flagship of the nearby Marstons' brewery.

The only pub in Grange Street has been the Star and Garter. Similarly, the Grange Inn has been the only one in Charles Street. Both have survived. There is just one public house in Shobnall Street today, and that's the Prince Arthur. The Locomotive Inn has gone along with the Britannia Inn and so has the only pub in Henry Street, the Outwoods Inn.

The Acorn Inn at Rough Hayes near Needwood just makes it into this book. Often referred to by the locals as the A'Cun, it has always been one of the most well-known public houses in Burton partly due to the free publicity it has received from the local buses. For decades, the destination board on the old Burton Corporation No. 10 heading up Shobnall Road read Acorn Inn. The old maroon buses may no longer be around, but the tradition continues to this day with the replacement service still terminating across

Above: The Mount Pleasant, usually known as Bessie Bull's after the name of the well-known landlady. It closed down in February 1961 after over 100 years in the same family. Standing on the bank of the canal at Shobnall, it was popular with anglers and crews of barges. This splendid drawing is by local artist David Wright.

Left: A commemorative tankard featuring Bessie Bull's based on David Wrights painting.

The Albion Hotel.

The Star and Garter as it once was.

The Grange in the early 1980s. A Bass house.

the road from the pub. Apparently an inn called the Royal Oak once stood on the site but, around 1866, Mr Greatorex of Rangemore had a new one built to replace it. What better name for a replacement for an oak than an acorn, a model of which still forms part of the apex of the roof? There is some evidence of a licensed premises called the Forest Arms, also in Rough Hayes and again owned by Mr Greatorex, although it is possible it may be the same inn.

For sixty-seven years, the pub was home to Alice Newey, one of the town's most loved characters. Landlady there from 1934-1973 and known affectionately as Alice of the Acorn, she succeeded her husband as mine host after his death. He'd had his name over the door for the eight years from 1926. Alice rarely employed any staff, her own family willingly carrying out the various duties associated with running a successful pub. During the war, the Acorn was popular with American soldiers based at Sudbury and legend has it that the pub, painted white, was used as a marker by pilots returning to base at the nearby airfield. For many years, there was no running water or electricity; it was by the light of oil lamps that Alice, a talented pianist, entertained her customers to a musical evening as she tickled the ivories.

A delivery at the Prince Arthur on the corner of Shobnall Street and Casey Lane in the early 1980s.

Despite the Church Hill Street sign on the front of this pub, The Anglesey Arms is actually in Bearwood Hill Road in Winshill. Also see page 89.

six

A Sporting
Theme

Sport, games, and public houses have always gone together. A century ago, skittles and bagatelle were amongst the most popular pub games. It is still possible for the slightly more energetic to get a game of skittles in a couple of Burton pubs. Shove halfpenny, dicing and something called 'devil amongst the tailors' were played too. Then came the likes of darts, dominoes and cribbage. These days, it is just as likely to be an hour or so on the pool table or an evening racking your brains to avoid humiliation in the ever-popular pub quiz.

Outside, it might be a game of bowls on a beautifully-manicured bowling green. At least six pubs in Burton had bowling greens at one time or another, such as The Anglesey Arms on Bearwood Hill Road and, in Stapenhill, the Gardens in Waterside and the Barley on Main Street, all three of which are still in use. Sadly, the others at the Albion Hotel, the Wyggeston and the Punch Bowl have been converted into car parks. There have been two pubs in Burton called the Bowling Green, one in Borough Road and the other in the Market Place. Not surprisingly, it is thought they may have had greens too.

Football and pubs are well linked, in fact many have had their own teams competing in local leagues and the Burton and District Football Association was founded in a pub, the Rising Sun in Horninglow Street, back in 1871. What better way was there for fans to drown their sorrows or celebrate a win than with a few beers in their local? A local like the Football Tavern situated near Burton Albion's Eton Park football ground, a pub popular with fans before and after matches.

Over the years, many well-known sportsmen have been tempted to try their hand at running a public house, some more successfully than others. Burton pubs have had their fair share. For a while, the name over the door at the Dog and Partridge in New Street was John David Stamps, better known as Jackie Stamps, the famous Derby County centre-forward whose two goals in the 1946 Cup Final helped the Rams to lift the FA Cup for the first and, so far, only time. He later played for, and then managed, Burton Albion.

HEADQUARTERS BURTON AND DISTRICT F.A.

When in

BURTON-ON-TRENT

VISIT

"The Fox & Goose"

BRIDGE STREET

★

MINE HOST AND HOSTESS :
NORMAN and EILEEN MACHIN

★

DRAUGHT AND BOTTLED BASS

CHOICE WINES AND SPIRITS

SITUATED NEAR NEW BARGATES SHOPPING
CENTRE AND BOWLING ALLEY

The Fox and Goose was the headquarters of the Burton and District Football Association. Here, Norman and Eileen Machin were exhorting visitors to call at the pub which they said was situated near to the new Bargates shopping centre and bowling alley. The pub is now the Bridge Inn, most of the shopping centre is boarded up.

Winshill bowlers and their families at the Anglesey Arms bowling green, in around 1960.

The Black Horse ladies darts team proudly displaying their trophies. Charlotte Ralley, the landlady, is sitting on the left of the front row. Sitting centre table is Faith Hudson, Charlotte's daughter who took over the pub following her mother's death in 1943.

Another man with a Cup-winners medal was Billy Rankin, the licensee at the Devonshire Arms. Described as a friendly and well-respected person, he was extremely popular with the football fraternity who frequented his pub. Born in Dumbarton, a giant of a man apparently, he was an outstanding centre-half playing for Dundee, Blackburn Rovers and Charlton Athletic. It was in 1928 whilst with Blackburn that Billy gained an FA Cup-winners medal when Rovers beat Huddersfield Town 3-1. In 1932, Blackburn were drawn against Burton Town in the third round of the FA Cup. Rovers were one of the outstanding teams in the country and the match caused tremendous excitement. It may well have been as a result of this match that Rankin joined Burton Town as player-manager in 1933.

Des Anderson, the ex-assistant manager to Dave Mackay at Derby, was the landlord at the Dog Inn in Lichfield Street. Their team won the First Division Championship in 1974-75. Hughie McLaren, the old Derby winger from the early 1950s who later played for Burton Albion, was the landlord at the Rifleman Inn in Derby Street.

Staying on a football theme, Billy Sneddon, who was appointed player-manager of Burton Albion in 1952 at the age of thirty-eight, later became licensee at the White Lion in Bank Square. Initially with Hamilton Academicals and then with Falkirk, he moved south to Brentford in 1935 and later became captain at Swansea Town before moving down the road to Newport County. Les Marshment, who played for Burton Town in the 1930s was landlord at the Star Inn, High Street as well as the New Inn and the Staffordshire Knot, both in Station Street, before taking over at the Marquis of Lorne in Uxbridge Street.

Football team from the Coopers Arms in Anglesey Road, *c.* 1978/79.

Above left: Billy Rankin, who kept the Devonshire Arms in Station Street, is with his Blackburn Rovers colleagues on a cigarette card issued by John Player & Son. He won an FA Cup-winners medal when the Lancashire side overcame Huddersfield Town 3-1 in the 1928 Final at Wembley.

Above right: The proprietor of the Union Hotel in Union Street, Albert E. Bates, was treasurer of the Burton Football Association and chairman of the Referee Committee too. It would be interesting to know whether Old Roger, the footballers' tonic, was consumed by the players before matches or afterwards, and was it the beer that was always in condition or could it have been referring to the footballers?

Right: Les Marshment was a well-known local sportsman, having played football for Burton Town in the 1930s. He kept the Star Inn in High Street, the New Inn and the Staffordshire Knot both in Station Street and finally the Marquis of Lorne in Uxbridge Street.

J.WEINBERG

Back in the 1930s, the Shakespeare in Victoria Crescent was the headquarters of Burton Town Football Club. This was just a reminder from H. Watson, the proprietor, that it was 'still the footballers' house' although it was also the H.Q. of the Burton Flying Club too. That's pigeons, not aeroplanes!

For many years, the landlord of the Swan Inn was Cecil Tate, the son of Fred Tate, an England cricketer who made his debut against Australia at Old Trafford in 1902. Fred Tate apparently dropped a vital catch and was bowled with only four runs needed for an England victory. He was never selected again. Later in the 1920s, Fred became coach to Derbyshire CCC before joining the Birmingham League club West Bromwich Dartmouth and, like Billy Sneddon, he was landlord at the White Lion in Bank Square. Cecil's brother was Maurice Tate, the famous Sussex and England bowler. For ten seasons, Maurice bowled slow off-breaks with little success but, after changing his style to fast-medium, he became one of England's greatest cricketers. Cecil himself, thirteen years younger than his famous brother, was no mean cricketer, a medium pace left-arm bowler turning out four times for Derbyshire in 1928 before later qualifying for Warwickshire, appearing six times for them in the early '30s. He also played for Burton Gentlemen where he was very successful.

Rather less well-known than the cricketing Tates was Robert Tinley, a first class cricketer who kept the Royal Oak in the Market Place around 1870. Earlier he had played fifty-four matches for Nottinghamshire, toured Australia in 1863/64 and later played for Burton Gentlemen as a professional. He was the leading exponent of 'lob' bowling in England and is buried in Burton cemetery.

The Albion Hotel has had numerous sporting connections. Rugby and golf were played close by and it was also the headquarters of the Shobnall Bowling Club. For eleven years, Frank Lee ran the hotel. He also managed the New Talbot Hotel in Anglesey Road and the Sportsman in Branston Road, played cricket for Worthington & Co. and later won the Breweries Cup with Marstons.

There is nothing many local cricketers enjoy more after a long afternoon in the field than a couple of pints and a chat. It provides them with an opportunity to quench their thirst, but perhaps more importantly, to mull over the day's events with team mates and, hopefully, a sprinkling of the opposition too. Many clubs have their own social clubs but for those which don't, it usually means a visit to the nearest pub, such as the Royal Oak, on Newton Road by the River Trent, which for generations has had strong connections with Winshill Cricket Club. Known to everyone as the Sump, it has now formally adopted that name. Boxing has been represented too. Around 1940, the landlord at Lichfield Street's Dog Inn was boxer Billy Jordan, who also coached pupils at Burton Grammar School. Pigeon clubs have had their headquarters in pubs, like the Red Lion in Horninglow and the old Shakespeare in Victoria Crescent.

Some 100 years ago when bagatelle and skittles were popular pub games in the town, it seems that quoits, a game normally associated with ships, was played in Burton pubs. A quoits team consisted of eight players split into four teams of two and, rather like bowls, the first pair to reach twenty-one were the winners. There were regular matches involving teams from various hostelries in the town.

Perhaps the strangest connection between sport and a Burton pub relates to the game of water polo. Back in the mid-1880s, meetings to draw up rules for the game were held in High Street's Star Inn where the landlord was James Mayger. As the game spread, the rules became the accepted ones and remain the basis of those in use today. Not only that, but the minimum measurement of the water-polo pool were those of the Burton public baths and, in 1889, when the English water-polo championship was established, Burton were the inaugural champions.

Sam Clewes, landlord at the Anglesey, sends down the first wood to mark the beginning of a new season in the late 1960s.

QUOITS.

BURTON AND DISTRICT ASSOCIATION.

FIRST DIVISION.

VICTORIA HOTEL v. WHITE HORSE (STANTON).

VICTORIA.		WHITE HORSE.	
F Davies	9	R Jones	6
W Twells	12—21	T Smith	3— 9
T Spencer	11	H Parker (A)	7
W Thompson	10—21	J Mansfield	8—15
F Thomas	14	W Illsay	4
W Odom	7—21	G Parker	8—12
J D Comrege	11	O Parker	8
G Hubbard	10—21	H Parker (B)	5—13
	84—		49—

NAVIGATION INN v. UNION INN.

UNION.		NAVIGATION.	
O Stone	13	G Skittrall	6
W Weighell	8—21	A Nelson	9—15
E Johnson	7	J Poole	8
W Thackwell	7—14	S Lord	13—21
T Dyche	6	C Jepson	16
T Ford	13—19	W Hatton	6—21
S Hodgkinson	13	J Whittaker	5
G Plant	8—21	H Elks	11—16
	75—		75—

GREEN MAN v. CROWN INN, STAPENHILL.

GREEN MAN.		CROWN INN.	
A. Arnold	8	H. Hathaway	11
A. Lang	6—14	J. Davis	10—21
W. Tooby	12	E. Woodburn	4
E. Tooby	9—21	H. Morris	3— 7
W. Letts	12	J. Fisher	5
A. Warren	9—21	G. Tooby	4— 9
E. Dyche	11	A. Lightfoot	6
R. Shires	10—31	W. Cooke	11—17
	77—		77—

SECOND DIVISION.

GRANGE INN v. LOAF AND CHEESE INN.

GRANGE.		LOAF AND CHEESE.	
E	7	J Kettle	7
W Gilliland	14—21	E Main	4—11
T Langton	8	J Wood	6
G Brown	13—21	A Street	2— 8
W Moss	6	A Henson	16
W Emmes	12—18	W Lawrence	5—21
F Gallimore, jun	14	H Eadd	6
T Perkins	7—21	J Street	3— 9
	81—		49—

GOLDEN BALL v. SHEFFIELD ARMS.

GOLDEN BALL.		SHEFFIELD ARMS.	
F Tew	14	H Fisher	0
E Shipley	7—21	B Geary	7— 7
J Quigley	13	J Orton	6
W Bateman	9—21	T Peach	9—15
C Chittock	10	T Beard	3
A Willis	11—21	F Orams	2 -5
W Clarke	10	W Wakling	6
J Tew	11—21	T Hitchman	4—10
	84—		37—

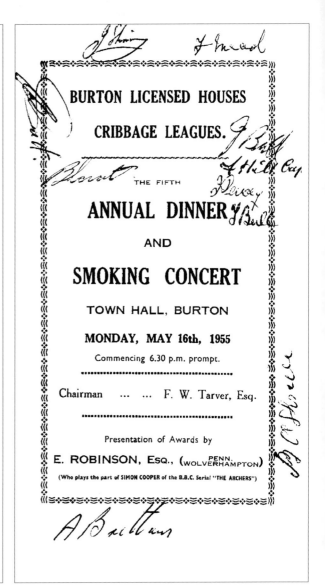

BURTON LICENSED HOUSES
CRIBBAGE LEAGUES.

THE FIFTH

ANNUAL DINNER

AND

SMOKING CONCERT

TOWN HALL, BURTON

MONDAY, MAY 16th, 1955

Commencing 6.30 p.m. prompt.

Chairman ... ... F. W. Tarver, Esq.

Presentation of Awards by

E. ROBINSON, ESQ., (WOLVERHAMPTON) PENN.

(Who plays the part of SIMON COOPER of the B.B.C. Serial "THE ARCHERS")

Above left: Dominoes, darts and crib have been the amongst the favourite pub games for many years but in the early twentieth century quoits was just as the popular. As can be seen from the newspaper cutting, the Burton and District Quoits Association had two divisions and there was a knock-out cup competition as well. It seems that a team consisted of four pairs of players and, rather like bowls, the first to reach twenty-one were the winners. Judging by the scores, again rather like bowls, it appears that the home side must have had some sort of advantage. It wasn't unusual for all four pairs of players to make maximum scores.

Above right: The Burton Licensed Houses Cribbage League awards ceremony not only took the form of an annual dinner, but was a smoking concert too. This notice was autographed by some of those taking part. The presentation of awards was by a Mr E. Robinson who, it seemed, played the part of Simon Cooper in *The Archers*.

seven

Up the Pub

Despite the changes in the leisure industry, increases in home consumption of beer and other alcoholic products, advice from various anti-drinking lobbies, not to mention a host of legislation and what appear to be an ever-increasing number of killjoys, a visit to the local is still a popular pastime. The plaintiff cry: 'There's nothing on the telly, I'm off up the pub' is still heard at the beginning of the twenty-first century. Although many pubs in Burton have disappeared, there are still enough to satisfy people. A few are newer houses, like the Bill Brewer and the Lord Burton, and there are sports bars, fun pubs and bar restaurants in the town centre. Thankfully, around eighty traditional Burton pubs remain. From the splendid old Plough in Horninglow is the Anglesey and the Sump in Winshill. All the way from the historic Acorn at Rough Hayes is the Elms and the Barley in Stapenhill and across town from the Blackpool Inn is the Derby Inn.

There are a handful of traditional pubs in the town centre: the Anchor, Devonshire, Roebuck, Dog, Leopard, Burton Union and the Bridge Inn. The Blue Posts is there too, although now a sports bar. The newer Lord Burton thrives and there's Yates's next door, but the other licensed premises in the town centre are mainly of the bar restaurant type.

Surprisingly, there are almost twice the number of public houses in Winshill and Stapenhill as there are in town. Despite various refurbishments over the years, most of them have retained their character, the Elms being a good example. There are plenty of pubs in Horninglow and Shobnall too, and particularly along Horninglow Road, where little has changed. Around thirty are our back-street boozers. Long may they continue!

One such 'back-street boozer' is the Coopers Tavern in Cross Street, one of the most famous pubs in Burton. For decades, it was a Bass house and it has always had the reputation of being one of the most interesting pubs in town. With its unique elevated bench seats in the bar, for generations it has been almost a second home to a host of local characters, many of them from the Bass brewery itself, as well as a sprinkling from further afield who fancied a pint or two from what was, in effect, the brewery tap. Imagine the astonishment when Bass sold it to Hardy & Hanson of Kimberley. Thankfully it

The last night of Bass at the Coopers Tavern, Cross Street. It wasn't safe to wear a tie!

BURTON-ON-TRENT

LICENSED VICTUALLERS'

ASSOCIATION.

OFFICERS.

PRESIDENT :

Mr. F. BRITTAN, "Grange Inn," Casey Lane, Burton-on-Trent.

VICE-PRESIDENT :

Mr. R. W. FAIRBROTHER, "William IV,"Church Gresley, Nr. Burton-on-Trent.

HON. TREASURER :

Mr. G. H. DYCHE, "Argyle Arms," Uxbridge Street, Burton-on-Trent.

COMMITTEE.

Retire 1946	Retire 1947	Retire 1948
G. H. DYCHE, "Argyle Arms," Uxbridge Street.	J. DAVIES, "Great Northern Inn," Wetmore Road.	G. E. SLEIGH, "Dog & Partridge," New Street.
H. MAXWELL, "Plough Inn," Stapenhill.	S. B. EDWARDS, "Eagle Hotel," Thornley Street.	R. W. FAIRBROTHER, "William IV," Church Gresley.
F. BRITTAN, "Grange Inn," Casey Lane.	A. E. BICKLEY, "Anchor Inn," New Street.	G. H. WIGLEY, "Loaf & Cheese," Waterloo Street.
J. W. FERN, "Waggoners' Inn," Horninglow Street.	B. B. WISEHEART, "Dog & Partridge," Tutbury.	R. R. LARNER, "Crown Inn," New Street.
T. BRADLEY, "Hanbury Arms," Sydney Street.	E. A. SALT, "Coopers' Arms," Wetmore Road.	J. ALBRIGHTON, "Roebuck," Horninglow Street.

SECRETARY :

T. W. DAVIS, Chartered Accountant, 18 High Street, Burton-on-Trent.

Above: The bar of the Thomas Sykes is something to behold. The walls are covered in memorabilia associated with local breweries and Burton Albion Football Club.

Left: Burton on Trent Licensed Victuallers Association, detailing the officers and committee for 1946.

The Coopers Tavern, 2004.

Truman's beer bottle labels.

continued to thrive with the help of draught Bass and the occasional guest beer. Now trading under the Tynemill banner, to the relief of its regulars its future looks assured.

The Thomas Sykes is also a favourite pub. Situated on the site of what was the Heritage Brewery, just off Anglesey Road, it is difficult to imagine a more traditional pub with its cobbled floor and whitewashed walls covered in brewing ephemera, and yet it has only been in existence for a few years. Created out of the stables and wagon house of the Heritage brewery when it closed in 1990, this cosy pub is run by one of its ex-employees.

Very little has changed in the bar and lounge of the Derby Inn, the old-fashioned friendly Marstons' house in Derby Road. Originally owned by Evershed's brewery, it is best described using a slogan favoured by Marstons' parent company, Wolverhampton and Dudley breweries: 'Unspoilt by Progress'. The landlord, Tony (Foggy) Foster has run the pub for over twenty years after taking over from his father. It is not just a pub either. For anyone in need of a couple of pounds of potatoes, a dozen eggs, even a link of black pudding as well as a splendid pint of Pedigree then the Derby Inn has long been the answer.

Another pub worthy of a mention is the Bridge Inn, the Burton Bridge brewery's first outlet, which opened in 1982. Their estate has now expanded and the Bridge's excellent beers can now be found at the Devonshire in Station Street, the Alfred in Derby Street and, more recently, the Great Northern in Wetmore Road. The cosy Old Cottage Tavern in Byrkley Street is the new name for the British Oak. Its impressive range of beers brewed, of course, by the Cottage Brewery situated in Hawkins Lane, remind Burtonians and visitors of the town's brewing heritage.

There is nothing pretentious with the outside of the Derby Inn, where little has changed over the years.

Two suspicious-looking characters in the Bridge Inn. David Moore, on the right, and Graham Coxon, waiting to be served.

A TOUR OF BURTON

In 1900 Mr A. Smith of Anglesey Road must have thought a walk round Burton upon Trent incorporating as many pubs as possible would be a good idea. This is the end result.

Strolling through the ORCHARD, accompanied by ADMIRAL BENBOW, I was surprised to meet WELLINGTON the hero of WATERLOO. He had just returned from PHILADELPHIA in a ship called the WHITE HART under the command of NELSON who saw to the WHEEL and ANCHOR and also boxed the COMPASS. During his travels he had visited the SMITHFIELD where he purchased a BLACK HORSE, a WHITE LION, a RED LION, a LEOPARD, a TIGER, a BLACK EAGLE, a LAMB, a BULL'S HEAD, a RAM'S HEAD and a WOOLPACK, which were intended as presents for the CORPORATION. The LABOURERS brought the WAGON and HORSES and took them to the STATION where they were conveyed by the MIDLAND on the RAILWAY to the CASTLE in the PARK.

When we arrived we found the FOREST GATE was locked so we opened it with the CROSS KEYS, and once inside we could see by the light of the MAN IN THE MOON and the SEVEN STARS that a combat was taking place in the GARDENS between GEORGE and the DRAGON. Turning round we saw the COACH AND HORSES coming over the RAILWAY BRIDGE by the DERBY TURN where PRINCE ARTHUR had been playing on the BOWLING GREEN together with PRINCE ALFRED, LORD NAPIER and GLADSTONE. All the time the DUSTY MILLER assisted by MILLWRIGHTS ARMS was pushing a PLOUGH obtained from a FOUNDRY in SHEFFIELD around the ROYAL OAK where it was guarded by a RIFLEMAN and a DOG. Just then the FOX AND GOOSE and the DOG AND PARTRIDGE were startled by the report of a GUN from an old SPORTSMAN who was on the OUTWOODS seeking to shoot a ROEBUCK grazing near the DEVONSHIRE ARMS.

Up came an OLD ENGLISH GENTLEMAN who picked up a GOLDEN BALL on his way and handed it to the CRICKETERS who threw it at the SARACEN'S HEAD but missed and hit, instead, ROBIN HOOD and knocked him between the BLUE POSTS and the BRIDGE into the river, and so doing disturbed the SWAN. He was fished out by the GREEN MAN and with the aid of the CARPENTERS ARMS was placed on the GREAT NORTHERN and taken to the UNION where he was attended by the MARQUIS OF LORNE and EARL GREY who made him WELCOME. As recompense for our trouble we received a ROSE AND CROWN which suggested refreshment. On our way to the GEORGE, the STAR shone brightly on the ALBION but we had found that the WHITE HORSE had fallen at the last fence so we adjourned to the MARKET HOTEL. Having ordered a FISH AND QUART and a LOAF AND CHEESE we put the juice of the VINE into a PUNCH BOWL.

Just then the BELL rang and we were informed of the arrival of QUEEN VICTORIA, the PRINCE OF WALES and DUKE OF YORK who were inspecting in the GUILD some pictures of ALMA, TRAFALGAR, ELEPHANT AND CASTLE, RAINBOW AND DOVE and a WHEATSHEAF tied in a STAFFORDSHIRE KNOT to the ELMS together with photographs of SHAKESPEARE and WARWICK. On leaving we were invited to the CRESCENT for a match between BLACKPOOL and BRANSTON to be attended by various MAYORS, BREWERS, ODD FELLOWS and FORESTERS. As NAPIER presented the winning team with a BRITISH CROWN we exclaimed WHO'D HAVE THOUGHT IT?

Other local titles published by Tempus

The Bands Play On! A History of Burton Bands
ERIC JOHNSON

This volume traces the history of brass bands around Staffordshire and Derbyshire from the late 1880s to the present day, and includes the input of many local people and organisations. The stories are illustrated with photographs and first-hand accounts and recall many local bands, including the Newhall Band, Tutbury Silver, Gresley Old Hall, Salvation Army bands, Uttoxeter Town and Derwent Brass, together with Burton bands.
0 7524 3079 3

Burton upon Trent Recollections
GEOFFREY SOWERBY AND RICHARD FARMAN

This selection combines archive material with local information to evoke a past way of life in this historic Staffordshire town. Special events are recalled, so too are the everyday lives of the people of Burton. The many previously unpublished photographs are supplemented by advertisements, wartime campaign leaflets, certificates and newspaper cuttings dating back over a hundred years.
0 7524 2642 7

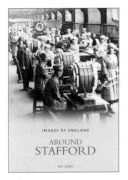

Around Stafford
ROY LEWIS

This book reproduces more than 200 photographs of Stafford and the surrounding villages of Gnosall, Haughton and Sandon. Their histories are examined along with changes that have taken place in local streets, buildings, schools, churches and factories. The area's social life is illustrated by events like the annual pageant, village sports meetings, royal visits and other special occasions.
0 7524 1811 4

Wolverhampton Pubs
ALEC BREW

This volume of archive images recalls the history of many of Wolverhampton's pubs, from the First World War through to the present day. Illustrated with over 200 photographs and postcards, this collection charts the changing facades of the town's pubs, from street corner pubs like the Hen and Chickens, to the imposing new pubs built between the wars, such as the Butlers Arms and the Black Horse, each serving a wider community than the old terraced pubs.
0 7524 3156 0

If you are interested in purchasing other books published by Tempus, or in case you have difficulty finding any Tempus books in your local bookshop, you can also place orders directly through our website

www.tempus-publishing.com